B R U C E
SPRINGSTEEN
C O M P L E T E

Copyright: © 1986 BRUCE SPRINGSTEEN
ISBN: 0-89898-469-6

Design: Sandra Choron
Associate book production: Folio Graphics
Front cover photograph: Paul Natkin
Back cover photograph: Neal Preston
Interior photographs: Neal Preston, except page 5, bottom, and page 7, Paul Natkin

CONTENTS

ADAM RAISED A CAIN

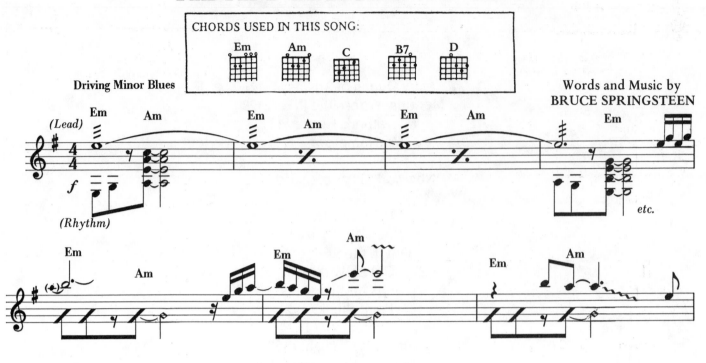

Driving Minor Blues

Words and Music by
BRUCE SPRINGSTEEN

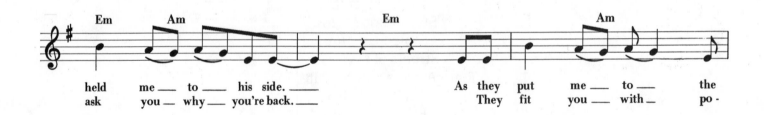

In the sum-mer that I ____ was bap - tized, my fa-ther
All of the ____ old fac - ces,

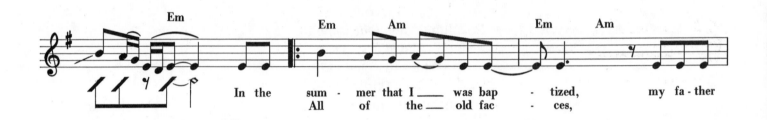

held me ____ to ____ his side. ____ As they put me ____ to ____ the
ask you ____ why ____ you're back. ____ They fit you ____ with ____ po -

wa - ter, he said how on that ____ day ____ I cried. ____ We were
si - tion, the keys to your dad -dy's Ca - dil - lac. ____ In the

pris-on-ers of love ____ a love in chains. ____ He was stand-ing in the door, I was
dark-ness of your room your mother calls you by your true name. You re- mem- ber the fac- ces the

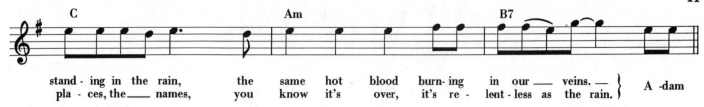

stand - ing in the rain, the same hot blood burn- ing in our __ veins. __
pla - ces, the__ names, you know it's over, it's re - lent - less as the rain. } A -dam

Chorus:

raised __ a Cain, __ A -dam raised __ a Cain, __ A -dam raised __ a Cain, __ A -dam

raised __ a Cain. __ raised __ a Cain. __ raised __ a Cain. __

Lost but not for - got - ten from the dark heart of a dream. A - dam raised a Cain, __ A - dam

Repeat and fade

raised a Cain, __ A -dam raised a Cain, A - dam raised a Cain, __ A - dam

Verse 3:
In the Bible Cain slew Abel,
And East of Eden momma he was cast.
You're born into this life paying.
For the sins of somebody else's past.
Daddy worked his whole life,
For nothing but the pain,
Now he walks these empty rooms
Looking for something to blame;
You inherit the sins,
You inherit the pain.

(Chorus:)

ATLANTIC CITY

Verse 3:
Well, I got a job and tried to put my money away,
But I got debts that no honest man can pay.
So I drew what I had from the Central Trust,
And I bought us two tickets on that Coast City bus.
Now, baby, everything dies, honey; that's a fact, *etc.*

Verse 4:
Now, I been lookin' for a job, but it's hard to find.
Down here it's just winners and losers and don't
  get caught on the wrong side of that line.
Well, I'm tired of comin' out on the losin' end.
So, honey, last night I met this guy and I'm gonna
  do a little favor for him.
Well, I guess everything dies, baby; *etc.*

BACKSTREETS

CHORDS USED IN THIS SONG:

G   Em   x D   x C   Am7   x Bm   D7sus

Words and Music by
BRUCE SPRINGSTEEN

Moderate Rock

One

Verse:

soft in - fest - ed sum - mer me and Ter - ry be - came friends, ___ try - ing in

vain to breathe the fire ___ he was born ___ in. ___ Catch - ing

rides to the out - skirts, ty - ing faith be - tween our teeth, sleep - ing in that

To Coda

old a-ban - doned beach ___ house, get - ting wast - ed in the heat. And

hid - ing on _____ the back -streets,_____ hid - ing on _____

_____ the back -streets,_____ with a love so hard and filled with de -

feat. _____ Run -ning for our lives at night on them back -

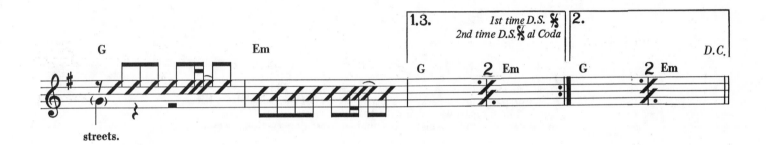

1.3. 1st time D.S. 𝄋
2nd time D.S. 𝄋 al Coda

2. D.C.

streets.

Coda

Af - ter all this time to find we're just like all the rest,

strand - ed in the park, and forced to con - fess to

Chorus:

hid - ing on ___ the back-streets, ___ hid - ing on ___

___ the back - streets, ___ where we swore for - ev - er friends, ___

___ on the back-streets un - til ___ the end.

Verse 2:
Slow dancing in the dark on the beach at Stockton's Wing,
Where desp'rate lovers park, we sat with the last of the Duke Street Kings,
Huddled in our cars, waiting for the bells that ring,
In the deep heart of the night, we could let loose of everything to go...

(Chorus)

Verse 3:
Endless juke joints and Valentino drag
Where dancers scraped the tears up off the streets dressed down in rags,
Running into the darkness, some hurt bad, some really dying,
At night sometimes it seemed you could hear the whole damn city crying.
Blame it on the lies that killed us, blame it on the truth that ran us down.

Chorus 2:
You can blame it all on me, Terry, it don't matter to me now.
When the breakdown hit at midnight, there was nothing left to say.
But I hated him, and I hated you
When you went away.

Verse 4:
Well, laying here in the dark, you're like an angel on my chest,
Just another tramp of hearts crying tears of faithlessness.
Remember all the movies, Terry, we'd go to see,
Trying to learn to walk like the heroes we thought we had to be. Well,

(To Coda)

BADLANDS

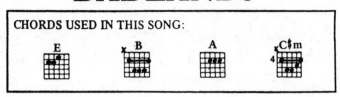

CHORDS USED IN THIS SONG:

Words and Music by
BRUCE SPRINGSTEEN

Moderate Fast Rock

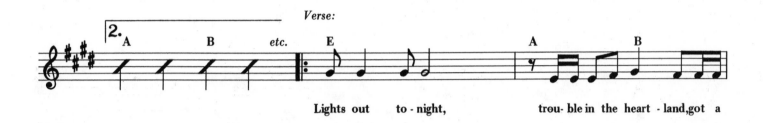

Verse:

Lights out to-night, trou-ble in the heart-land, got a

head on col-lis-ion, smash - ing in my guts, man, I'm caught in a cross-fire,

that I don't un-der-stand.__ (But there's one thing I know for sure, girl.)

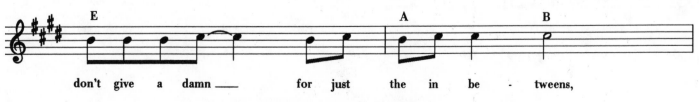

I don't give a damn __ for the same old played out scenes, I

don't give a damn __ for just the in be - tweens,

hon - ey I want the heart, I want the soul, I want con - trol right

now. ___ (You bet - ter lis - ten to me, ba - by.) Talk ___

*Bridge

___ a - bout a dream, try ___ to make it real. ___ You

wake up in the night with a fear so real, you

spend your life wait - ing for a mo -ment that just don't come; well, don't

Chorus:

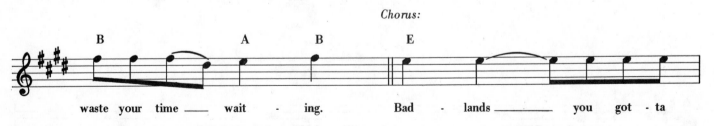

waste your time ___ wait - ing. Bad - lands ___ you got - ta

* Omit measures 17-24(Bridge) 3rd time through.

live it ev - ery - day, let the brok - en heart stand for the

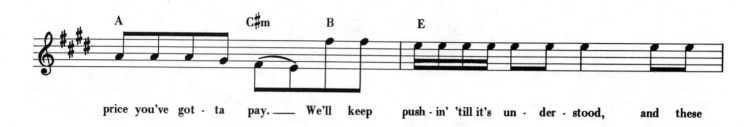

price you've got - ta pay. ___ We'll keep push - in' 'till it's un - der - stood, and these

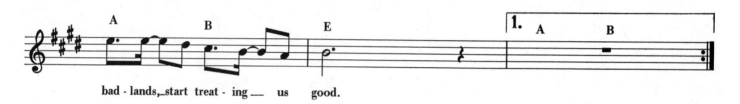

bad - lands, start treat - ing ___ us good.

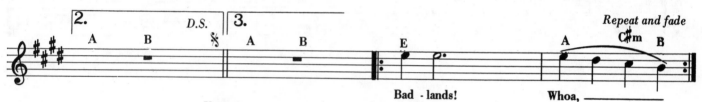

Bad - lands! Whoa, _____

Verse 2:
Workin' in the fields, till you get your back burned,
Workin' 'neath the wheel, till you get your facts learned.
Baby I got my facts learned real good right now.
(You better get it straight, darling.)
Poor man wanna be rich, rich man wanna be king,
And a king ain't satisfied, till he rules everything.
I wanna go out tonight,
I wanna find out what I got.

Bridge 2:
I believe in the love that you gave me,
I believe in the faith that can save me,
I believe in the hope and I pray that someday
It may raise me above these...

(*Chorus:*)

Verse 3:
For the ones who had a notion,
A notion deep inside,
That it ain't no sin to be glad to be alive.
I wanna find one face that ain't looking through me,
I wanna find one place, I wanna spit in the face of these...

(*Chorus:*)

BE TRUE

21

Coda

You say I'll___ be like___ those oth-er guys___ who

filled your head___ with pret-ty lies,___ and dreams that___ can

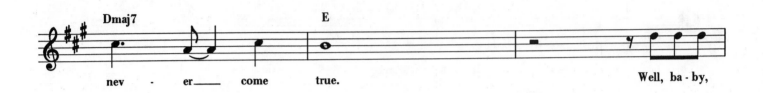

nev - er___ come true. Well, ba-by,

you be true to me and I'll be true___

to you.

Verse 2:
You see all the romantic movies, you dream and take the boys home.
But when the action fades you're left all alone.
You deserve better than this, little girl. Can't you see you do?
Do you need somebody to prove it to you?
Well, baby, you prove it to me and I'll prove it to you.

Verse 3:
In another cameo role with some bit player, you're befriending.
You're gonna go broken hearted looking for that happy ending.
Well, girl, you're gonna end up just another lonely ticket sold,
Crying alone in the theatre, as the credits roll.

(To Coda)

BECAUSE THE NIGHT

CHORDS USED IN THIS SONG:

Bm G A D C F#

Words and Music by
PATTI SMITH and
BRUCE SPRINGSTEEN

Moderate Rock

Take me now,— ba - by, here as I am.— Pull me close;— try and
Have I doubt— when I'm a - lone?— Love is a ring,— the

un - der-stand.— De - sire is hun - ger, is the fire I breathe.—
tel - e -phone.— Love is an an - gel dis - guised as lust.—

Love is a ban - quet on which we feed. — Come on now,— try and
here in our bed— until the morn - ing comes. —

un - der - stand the way I feel— when I'm in your hand.
(un -der your com - mand.)

Take my hand;— come un - der - cov - er. They can't hurt you now,—
(as the sun de - scends.) (touch)

24

can't hurt   you now,—   can't hurt   you now._____
(touch)   (touch)

Chorus:

Be -cause the night   be - longs   to   lov- ers.   Be-cause the night   be - longs   to   lust.

1.

D.S.

Be-cause the night   be - longs   to   lov-ers.   Be-cause the night   be - longs   to   us.

2.   *To next strain*   **3.4.5.** *Repeat ad lib and fade*

longs   to   us. With   longs   to   us.   love   we sleep;   with doubt   the vi -cious cir-cle

turns   and turns.   With - out   you I___ can -not   live,   for - give,   the

yearn - ing ,burn-ing, I   be - lieve   in time,   too real   to feel,   so

Repeat chorus & fade

D.S.S.

touch me   now,—   touch me now,—   touch me   now._____

BLINDED BY THE LIGHT

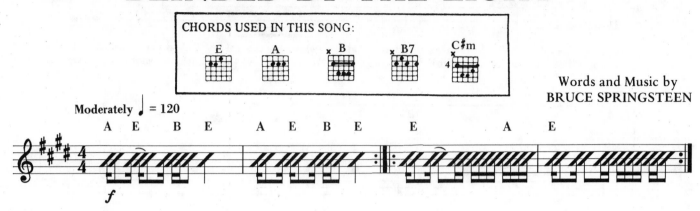

CHORDS USED IN THIS SONG:
E   A   B   B7   C#m

Words and Music by
BRUCE SPRINGSTEEN

Moderately ♩ = 120

Verse

Mad-man drummers bum-mers and In- -dians in the sum-mer with a teen-age dip - lo -mat.
all hot half - shot was head - in' for the hot spot, snappin' his fin -gers, clappin' his

In the dumps with the mumps __ as the ad - o -les-cent pumps his way __
hands. And some flesh - pot mas - cot was tied _____ in - to a lov -er's knot with a __

____ in - to __ his hat. With a boul-der on my shoul - der, feel-
what - not in her hand. And now young Scott with a sling - shot fi-

A   B7   E

in' kind -a old -er, I tripped the mer -ry -go -round. __ With this
n'lly found a ten -der spot and throws his lov - er in the sand. And some

ver - y un -pleas - ing, sneez - ing and wheez-ing the cal - li - o - pe crashed__ to the ground..
blood - shot for - get me-not whispers dad-dy's within ear - shot,save the buck - shot,turn up the band.__

1. 4. E

2.3.5. E

Chorus: A B

Some __ And she was blind - ed by the light.__
(he)

E A B E

__ Oh, __ cut loose __ like a deuce, __ an - oth - er run -ner in the night, blind -

A B C#m B7

__ ed by the light.__ She got down,__ but she
(He) (he)

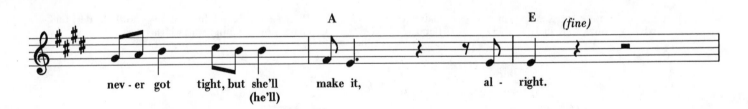

A E *(fine)*

nev - er got tight, but she'll make it, al - right.
(he'll)

A **1.** E C#m *D.S.* **2.** E C#m

Some

Bridge:

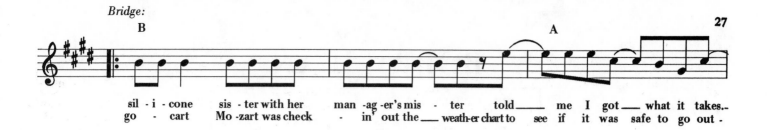

Verse 3:
Some brim-stone baritone anticyclone rolling stone
Preacher from the east, he says
"Dethrone the dictaphone, hit it in its funny bone,
That's where they expect it least."
And some new-mown chaperone was standin' in the corner
All alone watchin' the young girls dance,
And some fresh-sown moonstone was messin' with his frozen zone
To remind him of the feelin' of romance.

Chorus:

Bridge:

Verse 4:
Oh, some hazard from Harvard was skunked on beer,
Playin' backyard bombardier.
Yes, and Scotland Yard was tryin' hard,
They sent some dude with a calling card, he said,
"Do what you like, but don't do it here."
Well, I jumped up, turned around, spit in the air, fell on the ground,
Asked him which was the way back home.
He said, "Take a right at the light, keep goin' straight until night,
And then, boys, you're on your own."

Verse 5:
And now in Zanzibar a shootin' star
Was ridin' in a side-car, hummin' a lunar tune.
Yes, and the avatar said blow the bar,
But first remove the cookie jar,
We're gonna teach those boys to laugh too soon.
And some kidnapped handicap was complainin'
That he caught the clap from some mouse-trap he bought last night.
Well, I unsnapped his skull cap and between his ears
I saw a gap and figured he'd be alright.

Chorus:

BOBBY JEAN

CHORDS USED IN THIS SONG:

Words and Music by
BRUCE SPRINGSTEEN

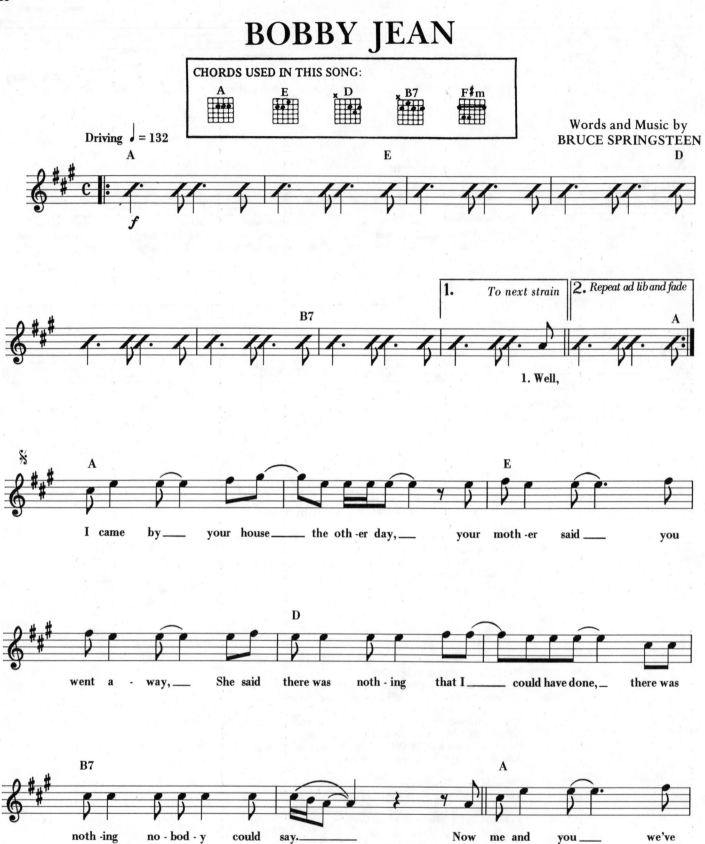

Driving ♩ = 132

1. To next strain
2. Repeat ad lib and fade

1. Well,

I came by ___ your house ___ the oth-er day, ___ your moth-er said ___ you

went a - way, ___ She said there was noth-ing that I ___ could have done, ___ there was

noth-ing no-bod-y could say. ___ Now me and you ___ we've

known each oth-er ev - er since ___ we were six-teen, ___ I wish

To Coda

I would-'ve known, I wish I could-'a ___ called you just to

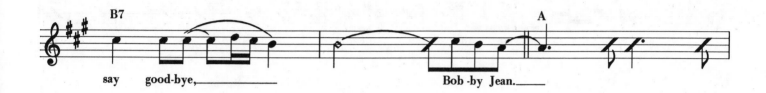

say good-bye, ___ Bob -by Jean. ___

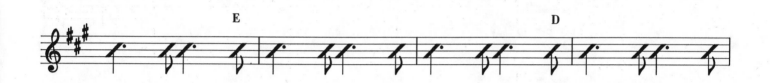

2.Now, you Now

we went walk - in' in the rain, ___ talk -

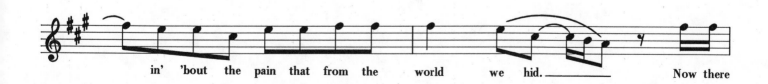

in' 'bout the pain that from the world we hid. ___ Now there

ain't no - bod-y   no - where,____   no how,____   gon -na

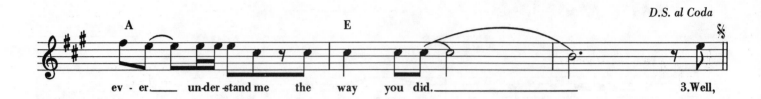

ev - er____ un-der-stand me   the   way   you   did._____   3. Well,

But   just   to   say   I   miss   you ,   ba -   by,

good   luck ,   good - bye,_____   Bob- by Jean.

Verse 2:
Now, you hung with me when all the others turned away, turned up their nose,
We liked the same music, we liked the same bands,
We liked the same clothes.
Yea, we told each other that we were the wildest things we'd ever seen,
I wish you would've told me, I wish I could've talked to you,
Just to say goodbye, Bobby Jean.

Verse 3:
Well, maybe you'll be out there on that road somewhere,
Some bus or train, trav'lin' along,
In some motel room there'll be a radio playin'
And you'll hear me sing this song.
Well, if you do, you'll know I'm thinkin' of you,
And all the miles in between,
And I'm just callin' one last time not to change your mind,
But just to say I miss you, baby,
Good luck, goodbye, Bobby Jean.

BORN IN THE U.S.A.

CHORDS USED IN THIS SONG:

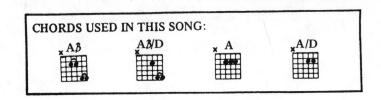

Words and Music by
BRUCE SPRINGSTEEN

Moderate Rock ♩=120

A(no3rd)

(instrumental) **f**

A(no3rd)/D

Verse:

A

Born down in a dead man's town,— the first kick I took was when I

A/D

hit the ground._____ End up like a dog that's been beat too much,— till you

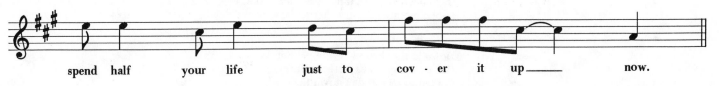

spend half your life just to cov - er it up_____ now.

Chorus:

Born   in   the   U.   S.   A._____   I   was

born   in   the   U.   S.   A.__   I   was   born   in   the

(Last time Fine)

U.   S.   A._____   Born   in   the   U.   S.   A.__   now.

Got in a little hometown jam,
So they put a rifle in my hand.
Sent me off to a foreign land
To go and kill the yellow man.

(To Chorus:)

Verse 3:
Come back home to the refinery;
Hiring man says, " Son, if it was up to me."
Went down to see my V.A. man; he said,
" Son, don't you understand, now?"

(To instrumental chorus)

Verse 4:
I had a brother at Khesan,
Fighting off the Viet Cong;
They're still there, he's all gone.

Verse 5:
He had a woman that he loved in Saigon,
I got a picture of him in her arms, now.

Verse 6:
Down in the shadow of the penitentiary,
Out by the gas fires of the refinery;
I'm ten years burning down the road,
Nowhere to run, ain't nowhere to go.

(To Chorus:)

BORN TO RUN

CHORDS USED IN THIS SONG:

Driving Rock ♩ =144

Words and Music by
BRUCE SPRINGSTEEN

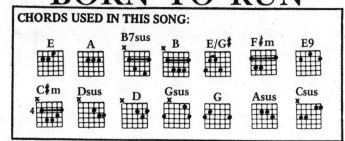

etc.

In the

day we sweat it out _____ on the streets of a run-a-way A-mer-i-can dream. _____

_____ At night we ride through man-sions of glo-ry in

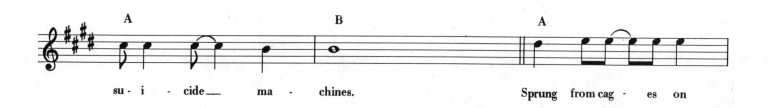

su-i-cide _____ ma-chines. Sprung from cag-es on

High-way 9, chrome-wheeled, fuel-in-ject-ed, and step-pin' out o-ver the line. _____

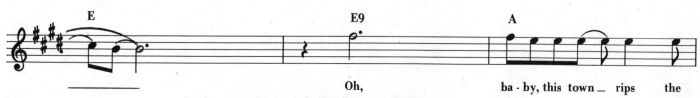

Oh, ba-by, this town _____ rips the

Verse 2:
Wendy, let me in, I wanna be your friend,
I wanna guard your dreams and visions.
Just wrap your legs 'round these velvet rims,
And strap your hands 'cross my engines.
Together we could break this trap,
We'll run till we drop, and baby, we'll never go back.
Oh, will you walk with me out on the wire?
'Cause, baby, I'm just a scared and lonely rider,
But I gotta know how it feels,
I want to know if love is wild, babe,
I want to know if love is real.

Verse 3:
The highways jammed with broken heroes
On a last chance power drive.
Everybody's out on the run tonight,
But there's no place to hide.
Together, Wendy, we can live with the sadness,
I'll love you with all the madness in my soul.
Oh, someday, girl, I don't know when,
We're gonna get to that place where we
Really wanna go, and we'll walk in the sun.
But till then, tramps like us, baby we were born to run.

CADILLAC RANCH

Words and Music by
BRUCE SPRINGSTEEN

Medium Rock and Roll

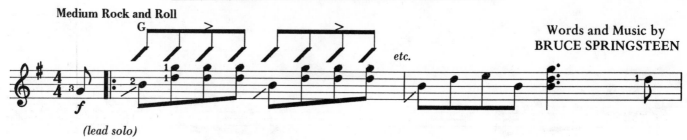

(lead solo)

There she sits, bud - dy, just a - gleam - in' in the sun, right
El - do - rado fins, great big white walls and the skirts: rides

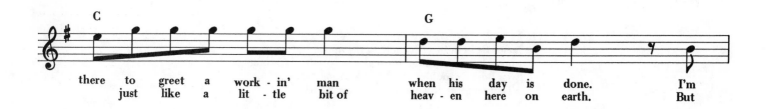

there to greet a work - in' man when his day is done. I'm
just like a lit - tle bit of heav - en here on earth. But

gon - na pack my pa and I'm gon - na pack my aunt; I'm
bud - dy when I die, throw my bod - y in the back. Ride

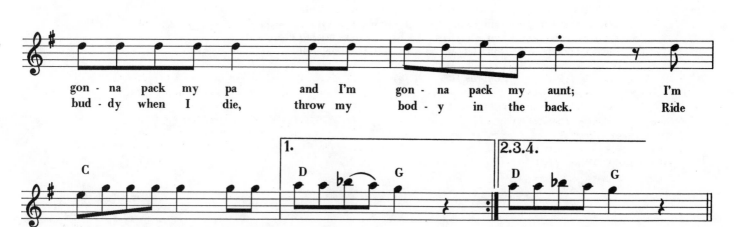

gon - na take 'em down to the Ca - dil - lac ____ Ranch.
me to the junk - yard in my Ca - dil - lac.

Chorus:

Ca - dil - lac, ____ Ca - dil - lac, ____ long and dark, ____

shin - y and black, o - pen up ____ your
(3) pulled up to ____

en - gines. Let 'em roar, tear - ing up the high - way like a
my house to - day, came and took my

1. *D.S.* 𝄋 **2.3.** *D.C.*
(last time al fine)

big old di - no - saur. big old di - no - saur.
lit - tle girl a - way.

Verse 3:
James Dean in that Mercury Forty-nine,
Junior Johnson runnin' through the woods of Caroline,
Even Burt Reynolds in that black Trans-Am,
All gonna meet down at the Cadillac Ranch.

(Chorus:)

Verse 4:
Hey little girlie in the blue jeans so tight,
Riding along through the Wisconsin night,
You're my last love, baby, you're my last chance.
Don't let 'em take me to the Cadillac Ranch.

(Chorus:)

CANDY'S ROOM

CHORDS USED IN THIS SONG:

Words and Music by
BRUCE SPRINGSTEEN

Moderately Fast Rock

Spoken: In Candy's room there are pictures of her heroes on the wall. To get to
city call my baby's number and they bring her toys. When I come

Candy's room, you gotta walk the darkness of Candy's hall.
knocking, she smiles pretty, she knows I wanna be Candy's boy.

Strangers from the

There's a sad - ness hid - den in that pret - ty ___

face, a sad - ness all ___ her ___ own, from

which no man can keep Can - dy safe. We

Verse:

kiss, and my heart's pump-in' to ___ my ___ brain, and the
ing, driv - ing deep in - to the night, I go

blood rush -es in —— my veins, ——
driv - ing deep in - to the light, ——
when —— I love Can - dy's lips. ——

We go driv - —— in Can - dy's eyes.
She says,

ba - by if you wan - na be —— wild,
you got a lot —— to ——

learn;
close your eyes, —— let them melt,
let them

fire,
let them burn. 'Cause in the dark - ness, there'll

be hid - den worlds — that shine,
when I hold Can - dy close—

—— she makes those hid-den worlds mine.

(Lead guitar solo with distortion)

She has fan-cy clothes and dia - mond rings,—
she has men who give her an - y - thing— she

wants, but they don't see, that

D.S. al Coda

what she wants is . . . . .

to - night.

Verse 2:
. . . me. Oh, and I want her so,
I'll never let her go, no, no, no.
She knows that I'd give,
All that I got to give,
All that I want, all that I live
To make Candy mine tonight.

COVER ME

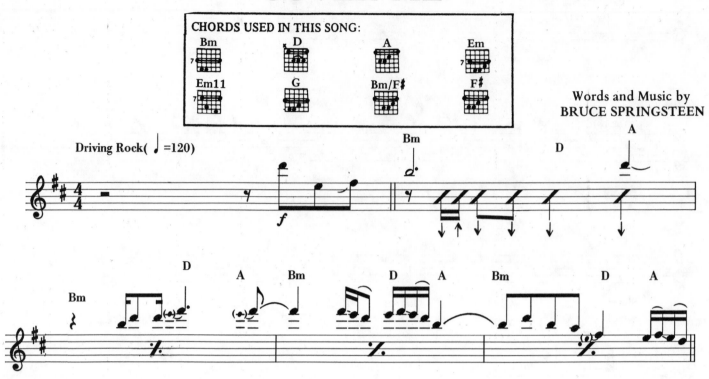

Words and Music by
BRUCE SPRINGSTEEN

Driving Rock (♩ =120)

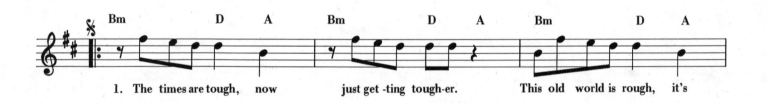

1. The times are tough, now just get-ting tough-er. This old world is rough, it's

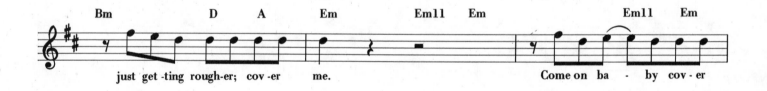

just get-ting rough-er; cov-er me. Come on ba - by cov-er

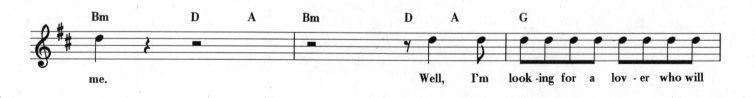

me. Well, I'm look-ing for a lov-er who will

come on in and cov-er me. 2.Now

Bridge:

Out-side's the rain, the driv-ing snow. I can hear the

wild wind blow - ing. Turn out the light; bolt the door. ___

I ain't go - ing out there no more. ___ 3.This there no more. ___ 3. This

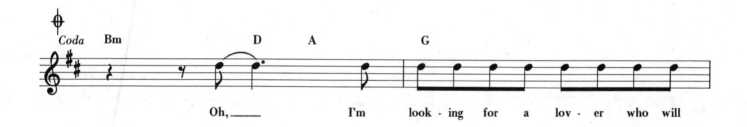

Oh, ___ I'm look - ing for a lov - er who will

come on in and cov - er me. Yeah, I'm

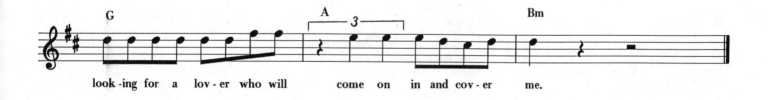

look - ing for a lov - er who will come on in and cov - er me.

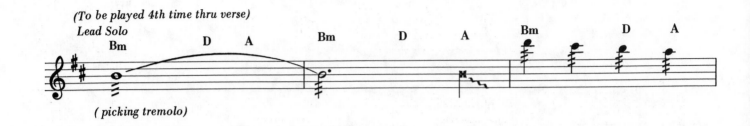

Verse 2:
Now promise me baby
That you won't let them find us.
Hold me in your arms:
Let's let our love blind us.
Cover me; shut the door and cover me.
Well, I'm looking for a lover who will
Come on in and cover me .

Verses 3 & 5:
This whole world is out there
Just trying to score.
I've seen enough;
I don't want to see anymore.
Cover me; come on in and cover me.
Well, I'm looking for a lover who will
Come on in and cover me.

Verse 4:
(Instrumental solo ad lib.)

CRUSH ON YOU

Words and Music by
BRUCE SPRINGSTEEN

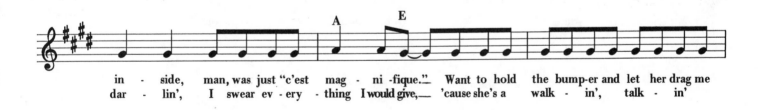

My feet were fly-in' down the street just the
spot a lit - tle stranger stand -in'

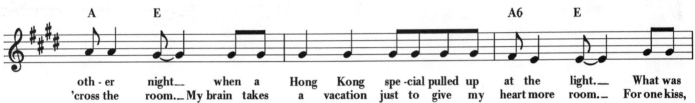

oth - er night.__ when a Hong Kong spe -cial pulled up at the light.__ What was
'cross the room.__ My brain takes a vacation just to give my heart more room.__ For one kiss,

in - side, man, was just "c'est mag - ni -fique." Want to hold the bump-er and let her drag me
dar - lin', I swear ev - ery - thing I would give,__ 'cause she's a walk - in', talk - in'

Chorus:

down the street.__
reason to live. }

Ooh, ooh, I got a crush on you.__

Ooh, ooh, I got a crush on you.__ Ooh, ooh, I got a

crush   on   you___   to-night.___

Some-times I

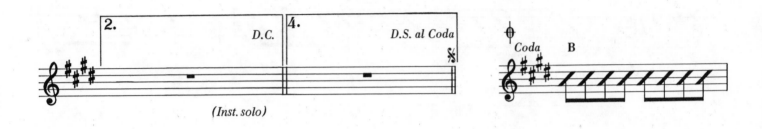

(Inst. solo)

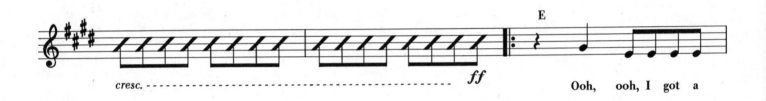

cresc. - ff

Ooh,   ooh, I   got   a

crush   on   you.___

Ooh,   ooh, I   got   a   crush on   you.___

Verse 3:
Well now, she might be talk of high society.
She probably got a lousy personality.
She might be an heiress to Rockefeller.
She might be a waitress or a bank teller.

Verse 4:
She makes the Venus de Milo look like she's got no style.
She makes Sheena of the Jungle look meek and mild.
I need a quick shot, Doc. Knock me off my feet,
'Cause I'll be mindin' my own business walkin' down the street.

(Chorus:)

DANCING IN THE DARK

CHORDS USED IN THIS SONG:

Words and Music by
BRUCE SPRINGSTEEN

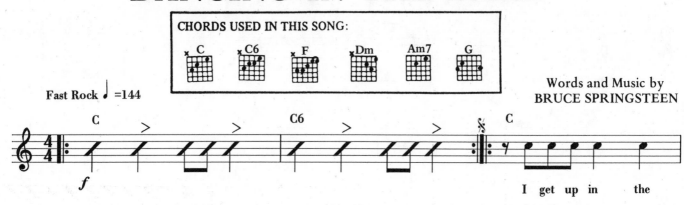

Fast Rock ♩ =144

I get up in the

eve - ning,   and I ain't got noth - in' to say.

I come home in the morn - ing;   I go to bed feel -

ing the ___ same way. ___ I ain't noth-in' but tired. _____

Man, I'm just tired and bored ___ with my - self.   Hey there

ba - by,   I could use ___ just a lit - tle help.

Chorus:

You can start a fire,_____ you can't start a

fire with-out____ a spark. _____ This gun't for hire _____

e - ven if we're just danc - ing in _____ the dark.

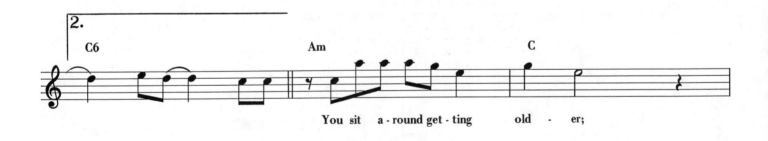

You sit a - round get - ting old - er;

there's a joke____ here some-where, ___ and it's____ on me. I'll shake this world off my

D.S. al Coda

shoul - ders.　　Come on　ba - by the laugh's ___ on　me. ___

Coda

danc - ing in ___　the dark.　You can't　start　a　fire ___

worrying a -bout ___　your　lit-tle world　fall-ing a - part. This　gun's　for　hire ___

e -ven　if we're just　danc - ing in ___　the　dark.

Verse 2:
Message keeps getting clearer;
Radio's on and I'm moving 'round the place.
I check my look in the mirror;
I wanna change my clothes, my hair, my face.
Man, I ain't getting nowhere just living in a dump like this.
There's something happening somewhere;
Baby I just know there is.

To Chorus:

Verse 3:
Stay on the streets of this town
And they'll be carving you up all right.
They say you got to stay hungry;
Hey baby I'm just about starving tonight.
I'm dying for some action;
I'm sick of sitting 'round here trying to write this book.
I need a love reaction;
Come on now baby gimme just one look.

To Chorus:

DARKNESS ON THE EDGE OF TOWN

CHORDS USED IN THIS SONG:

G   C   Em   D   Dm7

Words and Music by
BRUCE SPRINGSTEEN

Slowly

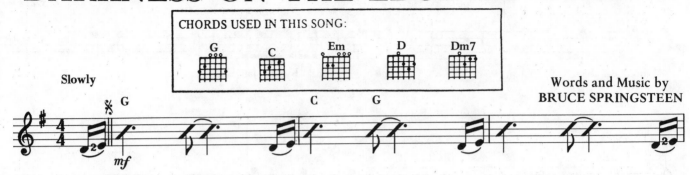

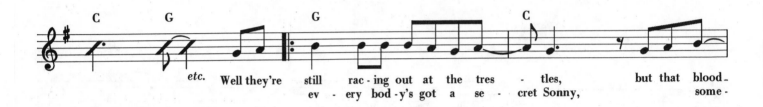

Well they're still rac - ing out at the tres - tles, but that blood
ev - ery bod - y's got a se - cret Sonny, some -

_ it nev - er burned in their veins, _ now I hear _
thing that they just can't face. _ Some folks spend _

_ she's got a house up in Fair - view, and a style _
_their whole lives try - ing to keep _ it, they carry it

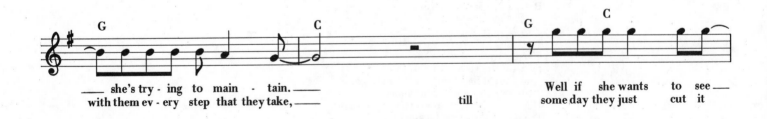

_ she's try - ing to main - tain. _ Well if she wants to see _
with them ev - ery step that they take, _ till some day they just cut it

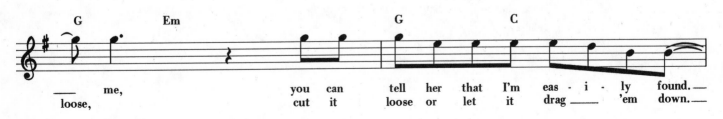

_ me, you can tell her that I'm eas - i - ly found. _
loose, cut it loose or let it drag _ 'em down. _

Tell her there's a spot out 'neath
Where no one asks an - y ques - tions or looks too

A - bram's Bridge, ___ tell her
long in your face, there's a dark - ness on the

edge of town, there's a dark - ness on the edge ___ of

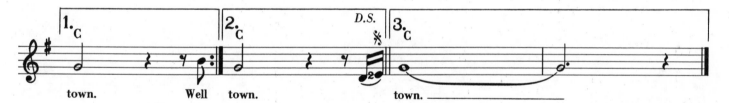

town. Well town. town. ___

Verse 3:
Some folks are born into a good life,
And other folks get it anyway anyhow,
Well now I lost my money and I lost my wife,
Them things don't seem to matter much to me now.
Tonight I'll be on that hill 'cause I can't stop,
I'll be on that hill with every thing I got,
Lives on the line where dreams are found and lost,
I'll be there on time ready to pay the cost,
For wanting things that can only be found,
In the darkness on the edge of town
In the darkness on the edge of town.

DARLINGTON COUNTY

eight hun-dred miles with-out see-ing a cop, we got rock-'n' roll____ mus - ic blast-

Chorus:

- ing off the T - top.____ Sing - ing, sha-la la sha

la la la la____ la; sha-la la la la la la.____ Sha-la la sha-

1. 2. **3.**

la la la la____ la; sha- la la la la la la. ____ la la la.____

* - Omit these 6 measures 3rd & 4th Verses

Verse 2:
Hey little girl, standing on the corner,
Today's your lucky day for sure, all right.
Me and my buddy, we're from New York City,
We got two hundred dollars, we want to rock all night.
Girl you're lookin' at two big spenders,
Why, the world don't know what me and Wayne might do.
Our pa's each own one of the World Trade Centers,
For a kiss and a smile I'll give mine all to you.
C'mon baby, take a seat on the fender, it's a long night.
Tell me, what else were you gonna do?
Just me and you, we could...

(To Chorus:)

Verse 3:
Little girl, sittin' in the window,
Ain't seen my buddy in seven days.
County man tells me the same thing,
He don't work, and he don't get paid.
Little girl, you're so young and pretty,
Walk with me and you can have your way.
Then we'll leave this Darlington City
For a ride down that Dixie Highway.

Verse 4:
Driving our of Darlington County,
I seen the glory of the comin' of the Lord.
Driving out of Darlington County,
Seen Wayne handcuffed to the bumper
Of a state tropper's Ford.
Sha-la la la la la la la;
Sha-la la la la la la.
Sha-la la la la la la la ;
La-la la la la la la.

DOES THIS BUS STOP AT 82ND STREET

Words and Music by
BRUCE SPRINGSTEEN

de - o. Tain - ed wom - en in vis - ta - vi - sion per -form for

out - of -state kids at the late show. still hope."

Sen - o - ri - ta, Span - ish rose, wipes her___ eyes and

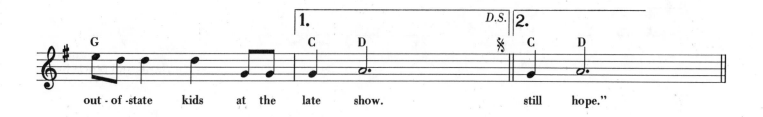

blows her nose. Up -town in Har -lem, she throws___ a rose ___

to some luck - y young mat -a -dor. ___

Verse 2:
Wizard imps and sweat sock pimps,
Interstellar mongrel nymphs.
Rex said that lady left him limp.
Love's like that (sure it is.)
Queen of diamonds, ace of spades,
Newly discovered lovers of the everglades;
They take out a full page ad in the trades
To announce their arrival
And Mary Lou she found out how to cope,
She rides to heaven on a gyroscope.
The Daily News asks her for the dope.
She says, "Man, the dope's that there's still hope."

DOWNBOUND TRAIN

Words and Music by
BRUCE SPRINGSTEEN

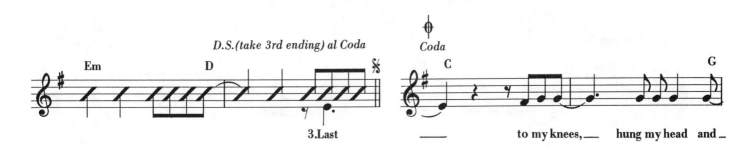

Verse 2:
She just said, "Joe I gotta go.
We had it once, we had it once,
But we ain't got it anymore."
She packed her bags, left me behind.
She bought a ticket on the Central line.
Nights as I sleep I hear that whistle whining.
I feel her kiss in the misty rain.
And I feel like I'm a rider
On a downbound train.

Verse 3:
Last night I heard your voice.
You were crying, crying, you were so alone.
You said your love had never died.
You were waiting for me at home.
Put on my jacket, I ran through the woods.
I ran till I though my chest would explode.
There in the clearing beyond the highway,
In the moonlight our wedding house shone.

Verse 4:
I rushed through the yard.
I burst through the front door.
My head pounding hard, up the stairs I climbed.
The room was dark, our bed was empty.
Then I heard that long whistle whine,
And I dropped to my knees, hung my head and cried.
Now I sling a sledge hammer on a railroad gang,
Knocking down them cross ties; working in the rain.
Now don't it feel like you're a rider on a downbound train?

DRIVE ALL NIGHT

CHORDS USED IN THIS SONG:

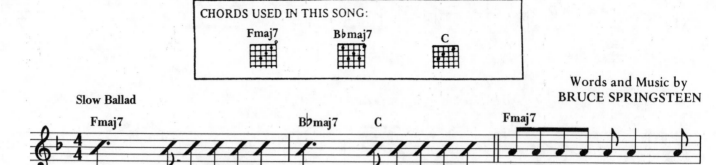

Fmaj7   B♭maj7   C

Words and Music by
BRUCE SPRINGSTEEN

Slow Ballad

When I lost you hon-ey some-

times I think I lost my guts, too.   And I wish

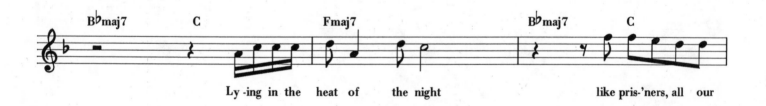

God would send me a word, __ send me some-thing I'm a-fraid to lose.

Ly-ing in the heat of the night   like pris-'ners, all our

lives, _____   I get shiv-ers down my spine, __ girl and all I

wan-na do is hold you tight. _____

Chorus:

I _____ swear I'd drive all night a - gain, just to buy you some

shoes and to taste your ten - der charms. And I _____

_____ just wan-na sleep to night a -gain in your arms. _____

Coda

wind, through the rain, the snow,the

wind, the rain. You've got you've got my, my love, oh,

girl, you've got my love, _____ heart _____ and soul.

Verse 2:
Tonight there's fallen angels,
And they're waiting for us down in the street.
And tonight there's calling strangers.
Hear them crying in defeat.
Let them go, let them go, let them go,
To their dances of the dead.
Let 'em go right ahead girl,
You just dry your eyes and come on, come on,
Come on, come on, let's go to bed.

(*Chorus:*)

Verse 3:
There's machines and there's fire, baby,
Waiting on the edge of town.
They're out there for hire,
But baby, they can't hurt us now,
'Cause you've got, you've got, you've got my love, girl.
You've got my love girl,
Through the wind, through the rain,
The snow, the wind, the rain.
You've got, you've got my, my love,
Oh girl, you've got my love, heart and soul.

FACTORY

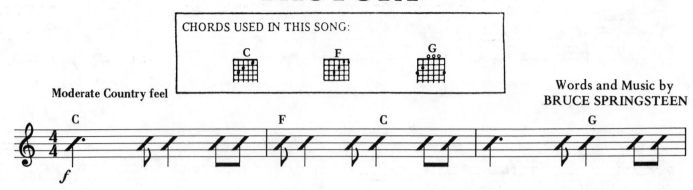

Moderate Country feel

Words and Music by
BRUCE SPRINGSTEEN

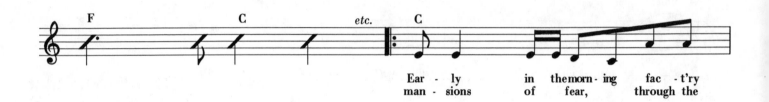

Ear - ly in the morn - ing fac - t'ry
man - sions of fear, through the

whis - tle blows, ___ man ris - es from bed and puts
man - sions of pain, ___ I see my dad - dy walk-ing through them fac - t'ry

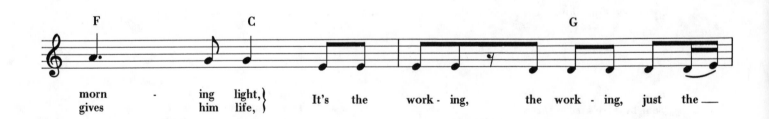

on his clothes. ___ Man ___ takes his lunch, walks out in the
gates in the rain. Fac - t'ry takes his hearing, fac - t'ry

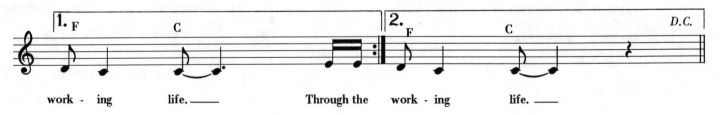

morn - ing light, } It's the work - ing, the work-ing, just the ___
gives him life, }

1. work - ing life. ___ Through the work - ing life. ___   2. work - ing life. ___

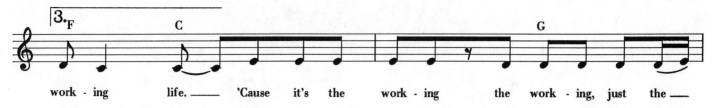

work - ing   life. _____ 'Cause   it's   the   work - ing   the   work - ing,   just   the __

work - ing   life. _____   Hmm. _____

Repeat and fade

Hmm. _____   Hmm. _____   Hmm. _____

Verse 3:
End of the day fact'ry whistle cries,
Men walk through these gates with death in their eyes,
And you just better believe boy,
Somebody's gonna get hurt tonight,
It's the working, the working, just the working life.

FADE AWAY

CHORDS USED IN THIS SONG:

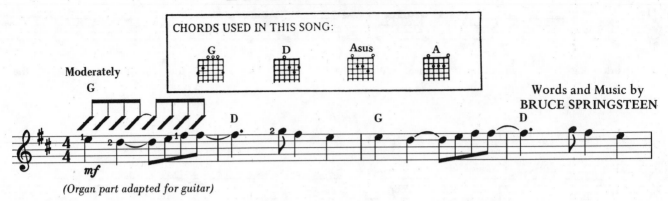

Words and Music by
BRUCE SPRINGSTEEN

Moderately

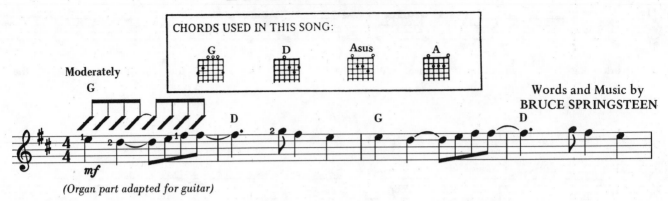

(Organ part adapted for guitar)

Well, now you

Now ba - by,

say you've found an - oth - er man who   does things to you that I   can't ____
say that you've made up your mind it's   been such a long, long, time   since it's been good with us, ____
I don't wan - na be ____ just an - oth - er use - less mem - o - ry   hold - ing you tight, ____

and   that no mat - ter what I do, it's   all o - ver now   be - tween
and that   some - where back a - long the line, you   lost ____ your love   and I
or just some   oth - er ghost out on the street to   whom you stop and po - lite - ly speak,

me and   you, ____ girl.   But I can't be - lieve what you say. ____
lost ____ your ____ trust.   Now rooms ____ that   once were so bright ____
when you   pass ____ on by, ____   van - ish - ing in - to the night, ____

No, I can't be - lieve what you say, ____   'cause ba - by,
are filled with the com - ing ____ night. ____   Oh, dar - lin',
left to van - ish in - to the night. ____   No, ba - by,

Chorus:

FIRE

Words and Music by
BRUCE SPRINGSTEEN

Moderately

(Bass part adapted for guitar)

(simile)

I'm rid- ing in your car, you turn on ___ the ra - di-
night, you're tak - in' me
et; Sam - son and De-

o. You're pull -ing me close,
home. You say you wanna stay,
li - lah. Ba - by you can bet

I just say no. I say ___ I don't
I say I wanna be a - lone. I say ___ I don't
a love they couldn't de - ny. My words ___ say

like it, but you know ___ I'm a li - ar.
love you, but you know ___ I'm a li - ar.
split, but my words ___ they lie. ___

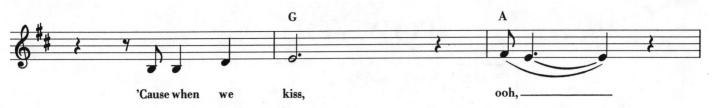

'Cause when we kiss, ooh, ___

(Fine)

fi - re. ___

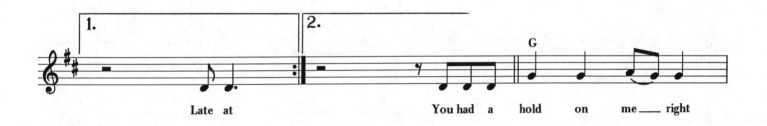

1. **2.**

Late at You had a hold on me ___ right

from the start ___ that gripped so tight I could-n't tear it a-part. My

nerves all jump-in'; act-in' like a ___ fool. Well, your kiss-es, they burn, but my

D.S. al fine

heart ___ stays cool. ___ Well, Ro-me-o and Ju-li-

FOR YOU

Words and Music by
BRUCE SPRINGSTEEN

Bridge I:

But you   let your blue walls — get in the   way of these facts. — Hon- ey,

odds.   Re - mem - ber how I kept you wait - ing when it was

my turn to be the god. _____

Verse 3:
Crawl into my ambulance,
Your pulse is getting weak,
Reveal yourself all now to me
Girl while you've got the strength to speak.

Verse 4:
'Cause they're waiting for you at Bellevue
With their oxygen masks
But I could give it all to you now
If only you could ask.

Bridge I(second time):
And don't call for your surgeon
Even he says it's too late.
It's not your lungs this time,
It's your heart that holds your fate
Don't give me my money, honey,
I don't want it back
You and your pony face
And your union jack;
Well take your local joker
And teach him how to act.
I swear I was never that way
Even when I cracked
Didn't you think I knew that you were . . .

Chorus (2nd time):
Born with the power of a locomotive
Able to leap tall buildings in a single bound?
And your Chelsea suicide with no apparent motive;
You could laugh and cry in a single sound.

(To Bridge II:)

Verse 5:
You were not quite half so proud
When I found you broken on the beach.
Remember how I poured salt on your tongue,
And hung just out of reach

Verse 6:
And the band they played the homecoming theme
As I caressed your cheek.
That ragged, jagged melody
She still clings to me like a leech.

Bridge I(third time):
But that medal you wore on your chest
Always got in the way,
Like a little girl with a trophy
So soft to buy her way.
We were both hitchhikers but you
Had your ear tuned to the roar
Of some metal-tempered engine
On an alien, distant shore.
So you, left to find a better reason
Than the one we were living for,
And it's not that nursery mouth
I came back for.
It's not the way you're stretched
Out on the floor,
'Cause I've broken all your windows
And I've rammed through all your doors
And who am I to ask you
To lick my sores?
And you should know that's true . . .

(To Chorus:)

FOURTH OF JULY
(Sandy)

Words and Music by
BRUCE SPRINGSTEEN

Verse 2:
Now, the greasers, oh they tramp the streets
Or get busted for sleepin' on the beach all night,
Them boys in their high heels, ah, Sandy, their skins are so white,
And me, I just got tired of hangin' in them dusty arcades
Bangin' them pleasure machines.
Chasin' the factory girls underneath the boardwalk
Where they all promise to unsnap their jeans.
And you know that tilt-a-whirl down on the south beach drag,
I got on it last night and my shirt got caught,
And it kept me spinnin', they didn't think I'd ever get off.

(Chorus:)

Verse 3:
Sandy, that waitress I was seeing lost her desire for me.
I spoke with her last night, she said she won't set herself
on fire for me anymore.
She worked that joint under the board-walk,
She was always the girl boppin' down the beach with the radio,
The kids say last night she was dressed like a star
In one of them cheap little seaside bars and I saw her
Parked with her lover-boy out on the ko-ko-mo.
Did you hear, the cops finally busted Madame Marie
For tellin' fortunes better than they do,
For me, this boardwalk life's through, babe,
You ought to quit this scene too.

(Chorus:)

FROM SMALL THINGS
(Big Things One Day Come)

Words and Music by
BRUCE SPRINGSTEEN

CHORDS USED IN THIS SONG:

Moderate Rock n' Roll

At six - teen she quit high —
late it was Fri -

— school, to make her for -tune in the prom-ised land.— She got a
— day he pulled in out of the dark.— He was

job be -hind the count - er in an all— night ham-burg - er stand.—
tall and hand - some; first she took his order, then she took his heart.—

She wrote faith - ful -ly home to ma - ma, " Now, ma-
They bought a house up on the hill - side, where lit - tle

ma don't you wor - ry none."— } "From small— things, ma -ma,
feet would soon run.—

70

Verse 3:
She packed her bags,
And with a Wyoming country real estate man
She ran down to Tampa
In an "El-Dorado Grande".
She wrote back, "Dear Mama,
Life is just heaven in the sun.
Well, from small things, mama,
Big things one day come."

(To Bridge:)

Verse 4:
Back home lonesome Johnny
Prays for his baby's parole.
He waits on the hillside
Where the Wyoming waters roll.
At his feet, and almost grown now,
A blue-eyed daughter and a handsome son;
Well, from small things, mama,
Big things one day come.
Well, from small things, mama,
Big things one day come.

GLORY DAYS

Words and Music by
BRUCE SPRINGSTEEN

Verse 2:
Well, there's a girl that lives up the block; back in school she could turn all the boys' heads.
Sometimes on a Friday, I'll stop by and have a few drinks after she put her kids to bed.
Her and her husband Bobby, well, they split up; I guess it's two years gone by now.
We just sit around talkin' 'bout the old times; she says when she feels like crying she starts laughin' thinkin' 'bout...

Verse 3:
Think I'm going down to the well tonight, and I'm gonna' drink till I get my fill.
And I hope when I get old I don't sit around thinkin' about it, but I probably will.
Yeah, just sittin' back tryin' to recapture a little of the glory of,
But time slips away and leaves you with nothin', mister, but boring stories of . . .

GROWIN' UP

Words and Music by
BRUCE SPRINGSTEEN

Well, I stood stone - like at mid - night sus -
pend - ed in my mas - quer - ade.____ And I combed my hair till it was
just right, and com - man - ded the night bri - gade.____ I was
o - pen to pain ___ and crossed by the rain, and I walked on a crook - ed

crutch. I strolled all a - lone ___ through a fall - out zone ___ and came

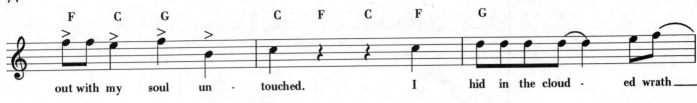

out with my soul un - touched.   I   hid in the cloud - ed wrath___

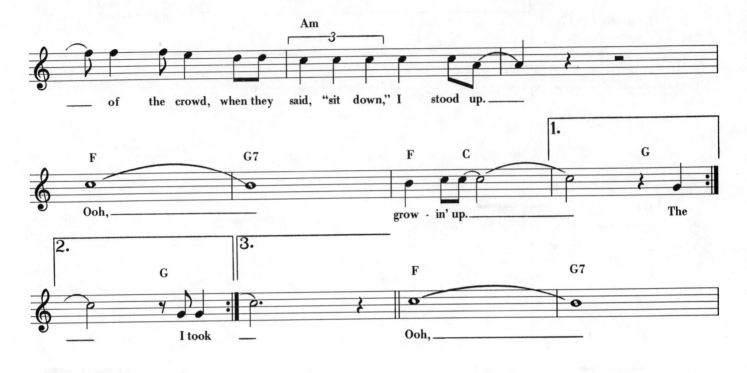

___ of   the crowd, when they said, "sit down," I   stood up.___

Ooh,___   grow - in' up.___   The

2.   **3.**
___   I took ___   Ooh,___

grow - in' up.___

Additional lyrics :
The flag of piracy flew from my mast, my sails were set wing to wing.
I had a juke box graduate for first mate, she couldn't sail but she sure could sing.
And I pushed B-fifty two and bombed 'em with the blues with me gear set stubborn on
    standing,
And I broke all the rules, strafed my old high school, never once gave thought to landing,
And I hid in the clouded warmth of the crowd, when they said, "come down", I threw up.
Ooh, growing up.

I took month-long vacations in the stratosphere and you know its really hard to hold your
    breath.
Swear, I lost everything that I ever loved or feared, I was the cosmic kid in full costume dress.
Well my feet finally took root in the earth, but I got me a nice little place in the stars
And I found the key to the universe in the engine of an old parked car.
And I hid in the mother breast of the crowd, when they said, "pull down,"
    I pulled up.
Ooh, growing up.

HELD UP WITHOUT A GUN

CHORDS USED IN THIS SONG:

Words and Music by
BRUCE SPRINGSTEEN

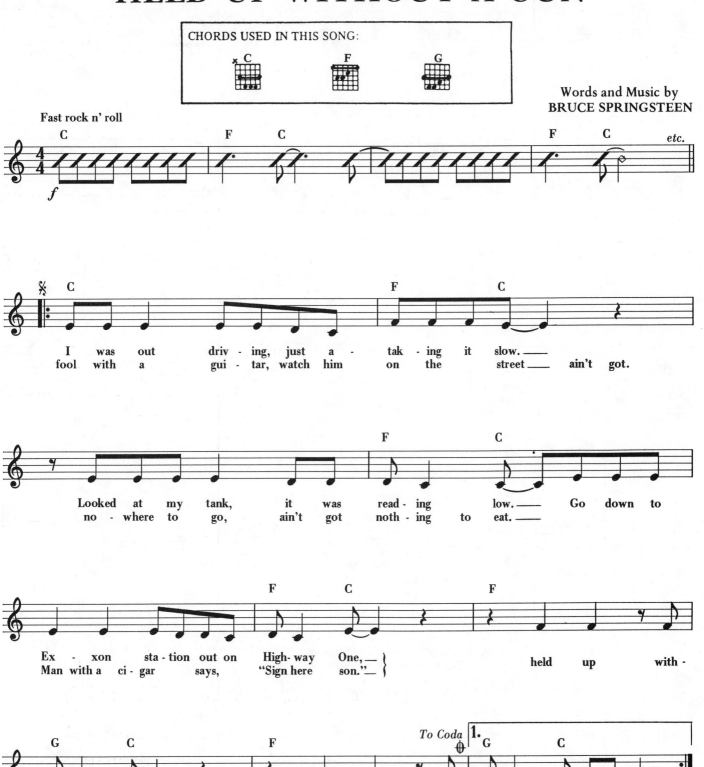

Fast rock n' roll

I was out driving, just a- tak- ing it slow. ___
fool with a gui- tar, watch him on the street ___ ain't got.

Looked at my tank, it was read- ing low. ___ Go down to
no-where to go, ain't got noth- ing to eat. ___

Ex- xon sta- tion out on High- way One, ___ held up with-
Man with a ci- gar says, "Sign here son." ___

out a gun, ___ held up with out a gun. ___ Some damn

out a gun. —

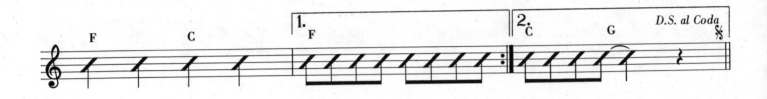

out a gun, — held up with -

out a gun, — held up with - out a gun. —

Verse 3:
Now it's a sin and it ought-a be a crime;
You know it happens baby all the time.
Try to make a living, try to have a little fun;
Held up without a gun, held up without a gun.

HIGHWAY PATROLMAN

CHORDS USED IN THIS SONG:

Words and Music by
BRUCE SPRINGSTEEN

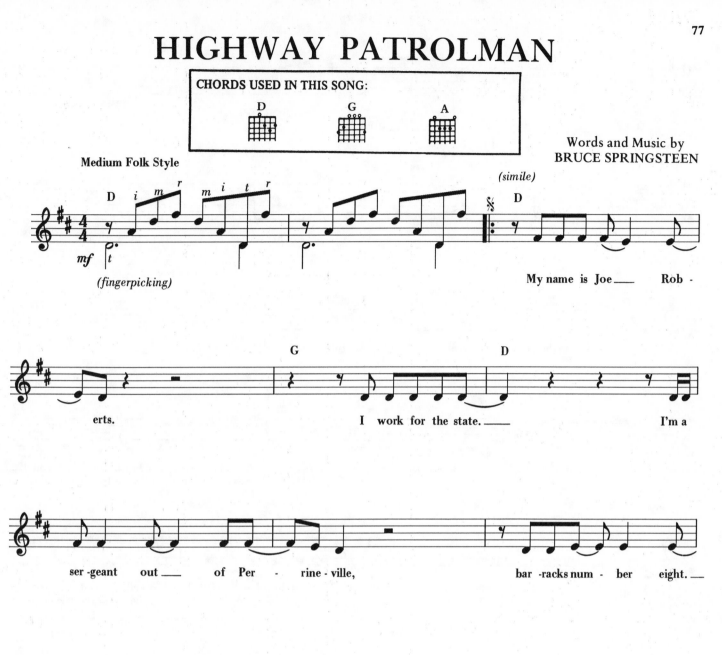

Medium Folk Style

(simile)

mf

(fingerpicking)

My name is Joe___ Rob-

erts.   I work for the state.___   I'm a

ser-geant out___ of Per-rine-ville,   bar-racks num-ber eight.___

I al-ways done an hon-est job,   I got a broth-er named Frank-

as hon-est as I could.___   I got a broth-er named Frank-

1.4.   **2.3.5.**

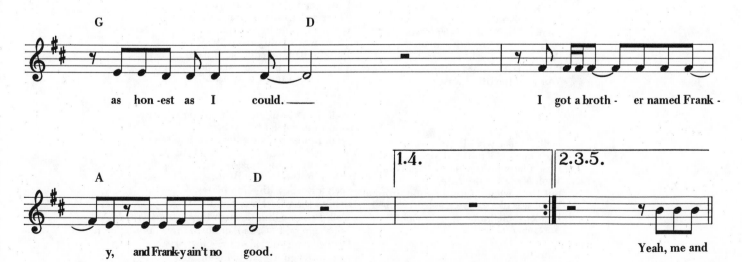

y,   and Frank-y ain't no   good.   Yeah, me and

Chorus:

Franky laugh - in' and drink - in'. Noth - in' feels —

— bet - ter than blood on blood. — Tak - in' turns — dan - cin' with Ma - ri -

a as the band played — "Night of the Johns - town Flood." I —

— catch him when — he's stray - in', { like an - y broth - er would. —
{ teach him how to walk that line. —

Man turns his back on his fam - 'ly, { well, he just ain't no
{ he ain't no friend of

1. *(fine)* 2. *D.S. al fine*

D.S. 𝄋 𝄋

good. }
mine. }

Well, the night —

Verse 2:
Now ever since we was young kids
It's been the same come down.
I get a call on the short-wave:
Franky's in trouble downtown.
Well, if it was any other man,
I'd put him straight away,
But when it's your brother, sometimes
You look the other way.

(Chorus:)

Verse 3:
Well, Franky went in the army
Back in nineteen sixty-five.
I got a farm deferment, settled down,
Took Maria for my wife.
But them wheat prices kept on droppin'
Till it was like we were gettin' robbed.
Franky came home in sixty-eight,
And me, I took this job.

(Chorus:)

Verse 4:
Well, the night was like any other.
I got a call 'bout quarter to nine.
There was trouble in a roadhouse
Out on the Michigan line.
There was a kid lyin' on the floor
Lookin' bad, bleedin' hard from his head.
There was a girl cryin' at a table,
And it was Frank, they said.

Verse 5:
Well, I went out and I jumped in my car,
And I hit the lights.
Well, I must-a-done a hundred and ten
Through Michigan county that night.
It was out at the cross-roads,
Down 'round Willow Bank,
Seen a Buick with Ohio plates.
Behind the wheel was Frank.
Well, I chased him through them county roads
Till a sign said "Canadian border five miles from here."
I pulled over the side of the highway
And watched his tail-lights disappear.

(Chorus:)

HUNGRY HEART

CHORDS USED IN THIS SONG:

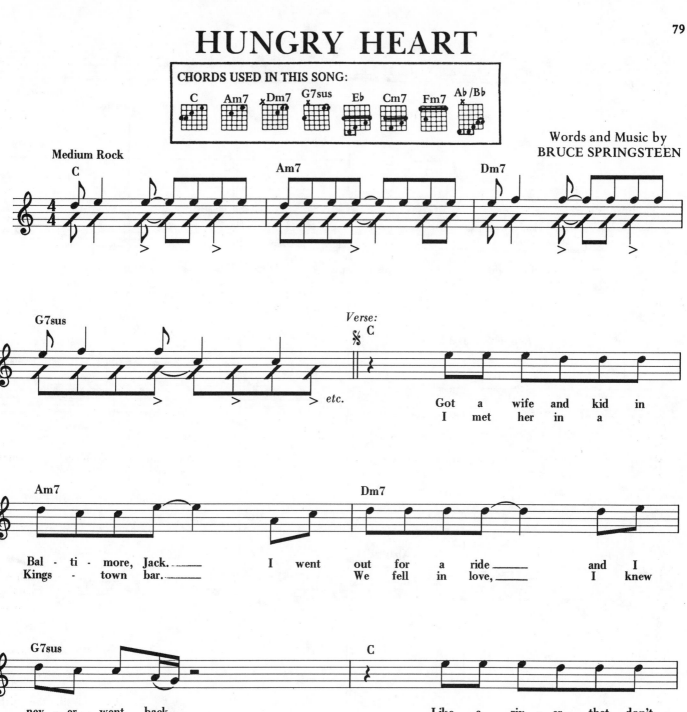

Words and Music by
BRUCE SPRINGSTEEN

Medium Rock

Got a wife and kid in
I met her in a

Bal - ti - more, Jack._____ I went out for a ride_____ and I
Kings - town bar._____ We fell in love,_____ I knew

nev - er went back._ We Like a riv - er that don't
it had to end._ We took what we had and we

know where it's flow - in', I took a wrong turn and I just kept go - in'.
ripped it a - part.___ Now here I am down in Kings-town a - gain.

Chorus:

Ev - ery -bod -y's got a hun -gry heart._ Ev - ery -bod -y's got a

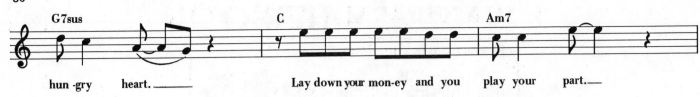

hun -gry   heart._____   Lay down your mon-ey and you   play your   part.__

Ev - ery - bod - y's got a   huh - uh - un - gry heart.   huh - uh - un - gry heart.

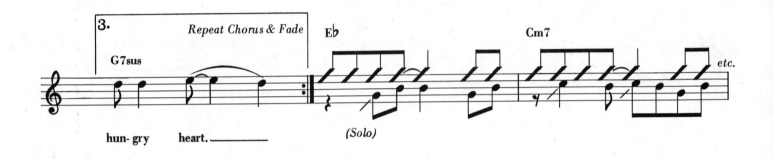

hun- gry   heart._____   (Solo)

Verse 3:
Everybody needs a place to rest.
Everybody wants to have a home.
Don't make no difference what nobody says:
Ain't nobody like to be alone.

(To Chorus:)

I WANNA MARRY YOU

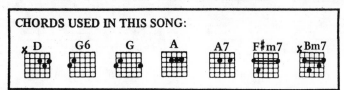

CHORDS USED IN THIS SONG:

D G6 G A A7 F#m7 Bm7

Medium Country Rock

Words and Music by
BRUCE SPRINGSTEEN

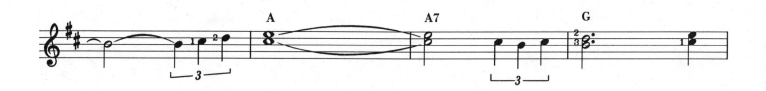

(organ solo adapted for guitar)

I see you walk-in' ba - by, down the street,—
You nev- er smile, girl, you nev - er speak.— You just

push - in' that ba - by car - riage at your feet.——
walk on by, dar - lin', week after week.— Raisin'

I see that lone - ly rib - bon in your hair.—— Tell me,
two kids a - lone in this mixed up world—— must be a

1.3.
am I the man— for whom you put it there?—
2.4.5. *Last time To Coda*
work - ing girl.
lone - ly life— for a

Chorus:

Lit - tle girl I wan -na mar -ry you. Oh, yeah!___ Lit - tle girl , I wan - na

mar -ry you.___ Yes, I do! Lit - tle girl, I___ wan -na

mar- ry you.___ My dad -dy said right be -

fore he died___ that true, true love was just a lie.___

He went to his grave a bro - ken heart.___ An un - ful - filled life, girl,

makes a man hard. Oh dar - lin',

Verse 2:
Now honey, I don't wanna clip your wings.
But a time comes when two people should think of these things,
Havin' a home and a family,
Facin' up to their responsibilities.
They say in the end true love prevails,
But in the end true love can't be some fairy tale.
To say I'll make your dreams come true would be wrong.
But maybe darlin', I could help them along.

(To Chorus:)

I'M A ROCKER

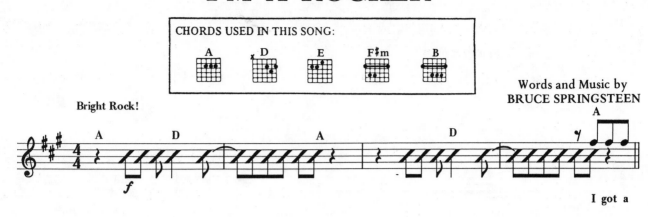

Words and Music by
BRUCE SPRINGSTEEN

Bright Rock!

I got a

Dou - ble - o - Sev - en watch; it's _____ a one and on - ly.
hang - ing from a cliff or you're tied to the tracks, girl;
fell for some jerk who was tall, _____ dark and hand - some.

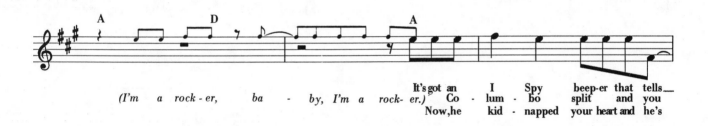

(I'm a rock - er, ba - by, I'm a rock - er.) It's got an I Spy beep-er that tells _____ Co - lum - bo split and you
Now, he kid - napped your heart and he's

_____ me when you're lone - ly.
can't find Ko - jak; *(I'm a rock - er, ba - by I'm a rock - er.)* true
hold - in' it for ran - som.

I got a
Well, like a

Bat - mo - bile so I can reach you in a fast shake,
love is bro - ken and your tears are fall - ing fast - er
Mis - sion Im - pos - si - ble, I'm gon - na go and get it back.

(I'm a rock - er, ba - by I'm a rock - er.) from the pain _____
When your world's _____ in cri - sis of an
in your heart, you have a
You know I _____ would-a tak - en bet - ter

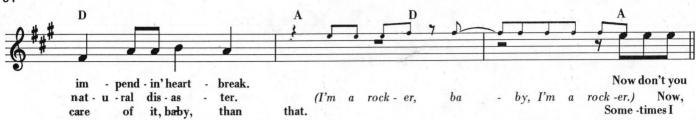

im - pend - in' heart - break.   Now don't you
nat - u - ral dis - as - ter.   (I'm a rock - er, ba - by, I'm a rock -er.) Now,
care of it, baby, than that.   Some -times I

call James Bond or Se -cret A - gent Man, 'cause they can't do it
I don't care whatkind of shape you're in. If they put up a road block, I'd
get so hot, girl,well, I can't talk. But when I'm with you,

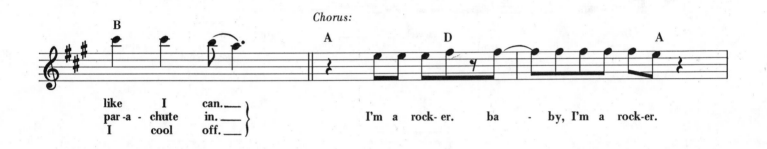

Chorus:

like I can.____
par -a -chute in.____   I'm a rock- er. ba - by, I'm a rock- er.
I cool off.____

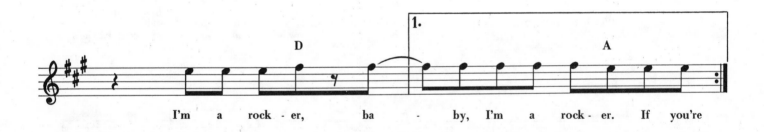

I'm a rock -er, ba - by, I'm a rock -er. If you're

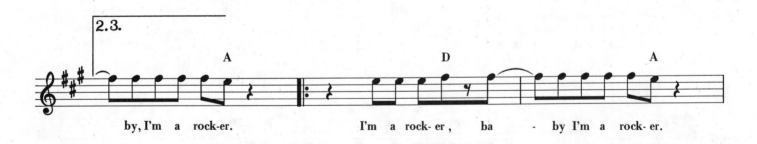

by, I'm a rock -er.   I'm a rock -er, ba - by I'm a rock -er.

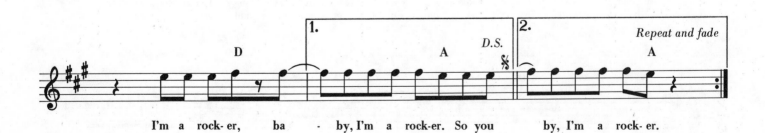

I'm a rock -er, ba - by, I'm a rock -er. So you   by, I'm a rock -er.

I'M GOIN' DOWN

Words and Music by
BRUCE SPRINGSTEEN

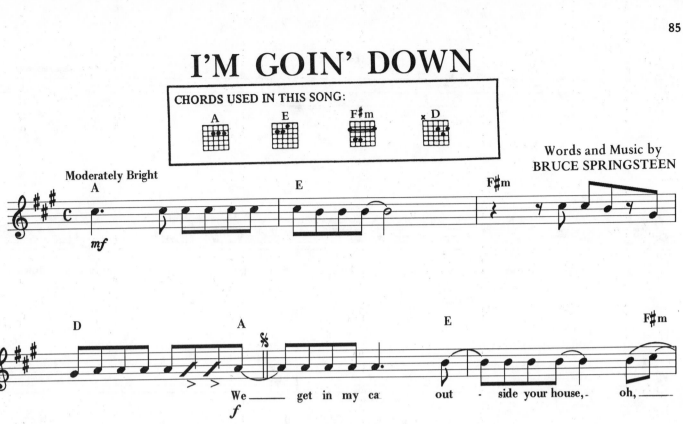

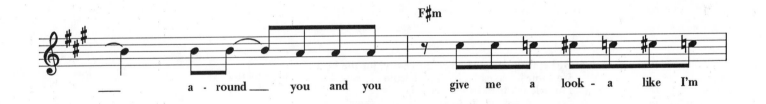

We ___ get in my ca out - side your house, ___ oh, ___

I can feel the heat a - com - in' 'round. ___ I go to put my arm ___

___ a - round ___ you and you give me a look - a like I'm

way out of bounds. ___ Well, ___ you let out one of your ___

___ bored sighs. Well, late - ly when I look in - to your eyes ___ I'm go - in'

86

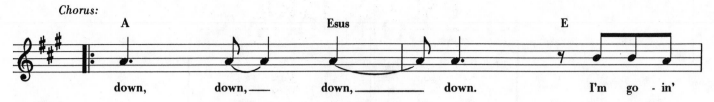

Verse 2:
We get really dressed up go out, baby, for the night.
We come home early, burnin', burnin', burnin', burnin' in some fire fight.
I'm sick and tired of your settin' me up,
Settin' me up, just to knock-a knock-a knock-a me . . .

(To Chorus:)

Verse 3:
I pull close now baby, but when we kiss, I can feel a doubt.
I remember when we started,
My kisses used to turn you inside out.
I used to drive you to work in the morning;
Friday night I'd drive you all around.
You used to love to drive me wild, yeah!
But lately, girl, you get your kicks from just a-drivin' me . . .

(To Chorus:)

I'M ON FIRE

CHORDS USED IN THIS SONG:

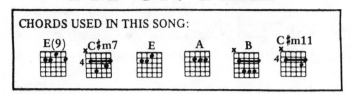

Words and Music by
BRUCE SPRINGSTEEN

Moderately Fast, with an easy flow

1.Hey, _____ lit - tle girl, is your dad - dy home?_ Did he

go a - way and leave you all a - lone?

I got a bad de - sire. Oh, _____ I'm on

fire!   2. Tell_

Some-times_ it's like, some-one took a knife, ba - by, edg - y and dull,_ and cut a

E   C#m7

six - inch val - ley through the mid -dle of my soul._

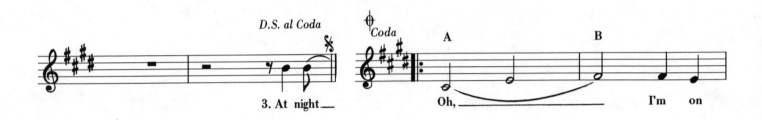

D.S. al Coda   Coda   A   B

3. At night_   Oh,_   I'm on

E   C#m11

fire!

Repeat ad lib and fade

E

Verse 2:
Tell me now, baby, is he good to you?
Can he do to you the things that I do?
I can take you higher.
Oh, I'm on fire!

Verse 3:
At night I wake up with the sheets soaking wet
And a freight train running through the middle of my head.
Only you can cool my desire.
Oh, I'm on fire!

INCIDENT ON 57TH STREET

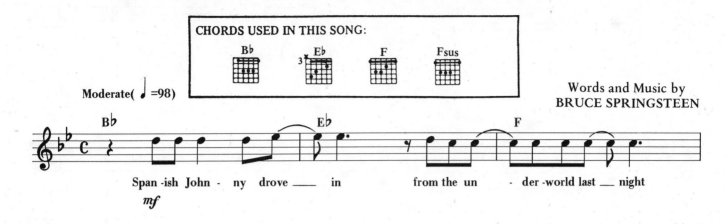

CHORDS USED IN THIS SONG:

Bb   Eb   F   Fsus

Words and Music by
BRUCE SPRINGSTEEN

Moderate (♩=98)

Span-ish John - ny drove ___ in   from the un - der -world last ___ night

mf

with bruised arms ___ and bro - ken rhy -thm and a   beat up old   Bu - ick   but

dressed   just like   dy -na - mite.   He tried   sell -in' his heart ___ to the hard ___

___ girls o - ver on eas - y street,   but they ___ sigh,

"John-ny, it   falls a - part   so   eas - y   and you know   hearts   these days   are

cheap".   And the   pimps   swung their ax - es and   said,   "John - ny   you're a

cheat - er." Well, the pimps___ swung their ax - es and said___

"John - ny, you're a li - ar." And from

out of the shad-ows___ came a young girl's voice said, "John-ny,don't

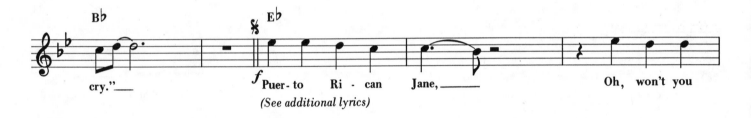

cry."___ Puer - to Ri - can Jane,___ Oh, won't you
(See additional lyrics)

tell me what's your name._____ I want to drive you down___ to the oth -

er side of town where par - a dise ain't so crowd - ed there'll be

ac - tion go - in' down on Shan - ty Lane to - night. All them gold -

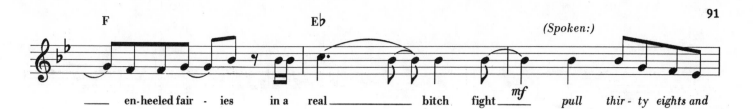

_____ en-heeled fair - ies   in a   real _____ bitch fight   _mf_   pull   thir - ty eights and

kiss   the girls   good - night.   Oh, __   Good - night, __ it's

al - right,   Jane. _____   Now __ let them black boys __

in   to light the soul _____ flame.   We may   find it out __ on the

street to-night,   ba   -   by,   or   we may walk __ un - til _____ the day - light,

may - be.   Well, like a   She whis - pered, "Spa-nish John-ny, you can leave me to - night, __

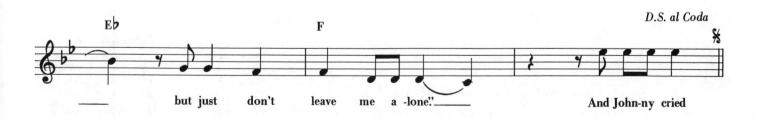

_____   but just   don't   leave   me a - lone." _____   And John-ny cried

Coda

Jane moves o - ver to share her pil-low but o -pens her eyes___ to see John - ny up and

put - tin' his clothes on. She says, ___ "Those ro - man -tic young ___ boys ___

All they ev - er want to do is fight. Those ro -

man -tic young boys, ___ they're call -in' through the win-dow: "Hey,

Span - ish John - ny, ___ you want to make a lit - tle eas - y mon-ey to -

night?" And John - ny whis - pered:

"Good - night,__ it's {all tight / al - right} Jane. I'll

meet you to-mor-row night on Lov-er's Lane._____ We may

find it out__ on the street to-night ba - by. Or

Repeat and fade

we may walk__ un - til ____ the day -light may - be." Ah, _____

Additional Lyrics:

Well, like a cool Romeo he made his moves, oh she looked so fine.
Like a late Juliet she knew he's never be true, but then she didn't really mind.
Upstairs a band was playin', the singer was singin' somethin' about going home.
She whispered, "Spanish Johnny, you can leave me tonight, but just don't leave me alone."

And Johnny cried, "Puerto Rican Jane, word is down the cops have found the vein."
Oh, them barefoot boys they left their homes for the woods,
Them little barefoot street boys, they said homes ain't no good.
They left the corners, threw away all their switchblade knives, and kissed each other goodbye.

Johnny was sittin' on the fire escape watchin' the kids playin' down the street.
He called down, "Hey, little heroes, summer's long, but I guess it ain't very sweet around here anymore."
Janey sleeps in sheets damp with sweat, Johnny sits up alone and watches her dream on dream on.
And the sister prays for lost souls, then breaks down in the chapel after everyone's gone.

(To Coda)

INDEPENDENCE DAY

CHORDS USED IN THIS SONG:

G   D   A

Words and Music by
BRUCE SPRINGSTEEN

Moderate Folk Style
(Capo 3rd fret)

(fingerpicking)

To Coda

(simile)

Verse:

Pa-pa ,go to bed now; it's get - ting late. Noth-ing we can
dark-ness of this house has got the best of us. There's a

say is gon-na change an - y - thing now._____ I'll be leav -
dark - ness in this town that's got us too._____ But they can't

ing in_____ the morn - ing from St. Mar - ry's gate.____ We would-n't
touch me now and you can't touch me now.____ They ain't gon- na

change this thing e -ven if we could some - how. 'Cause the
do to me what I watched them do to you. So

Chorus:

say good -bye.__ It's In - de - pend-ence Day.__ It's In - de - pend -ence Day__ all down the

line.____ Just say good -bye.__ It's In - pend-ence Day.__ It's In - de -

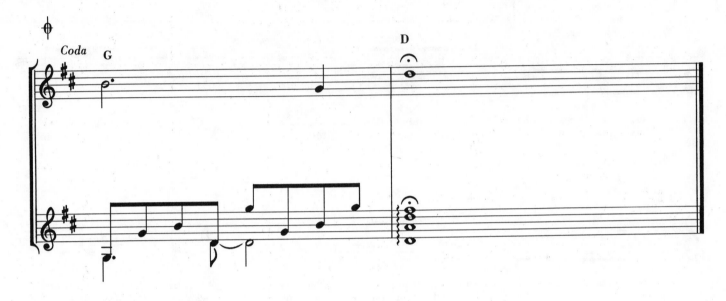

Verse 3:
Now I don't know what it always was with us.
We chose the words, and yeah, we drew the lines.
There was just no way this house could hold the two of us.
I guess that we were just too much of the same kind.

Chorus II:
Well, say good-bye. It's Independence Day.
It's Independence Day. All boys must run away.
So say good-bye. It's Independence Day.
All men must make their way come Independence Day.

Verse 4:
Now the rooms are all empty down at Frankie's joint,
And the highway, she's deserted clear down to Breaker's Point.
There's a lot of people leaving town, now, leaving their friends, their homes.
At night they walk that dark and dusty highway all alone.

Verse 5:
Well, Papa go to bed now; it's getting late.
Nothing we can say can change anything now.
Because there's just different people coming down here now
And they see things in different ways.
And soon everything we've known will just be swept away.

Chorus III:
So say good-bye. It's Independence Day.
Papa, now I know the things you wanted that you could not say.
But won't you just say good-bye? It's Independence Day.
I swear I never meant to take those things away.

IT'S HARD TO BE A SAINT IN THE CITY

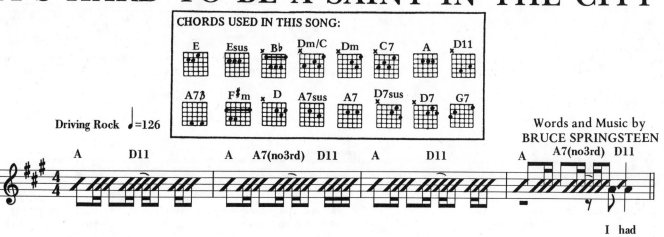

Driving Rock ♩=126

Words and Music by
BRUCE SPRINGSTEEN

I had

skin like leath-er and the dia-mond hard look of a co-bra.
King of the al-ley, ma-ma, I could talk some trash.

I was born blue and weath-ered, but I burst just like a su-per
I was the prince of the pau-pers, crowned down-town at the beg-gars

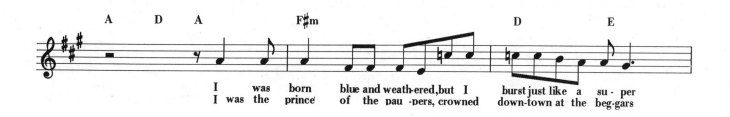

no - va. But I could walk like Bran-do right
bash. I was the pimp's main proph-et, I kept

in-to the sun,— dance— just like a Ca-sa-no - va.
ev-ery-thing cool,— just a back-street gambler with the luck to lose.

With my black-jack and jack-et and hair slicked sweet,— sil-ver
And when the heat came down and it was left on the ground,

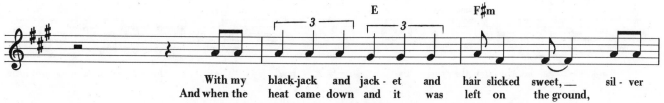

on by just a thread, but it's too hot in these tun-nels, you can get hit

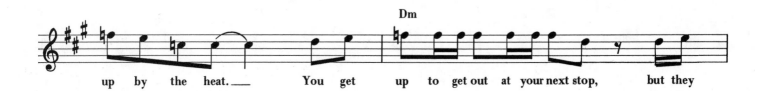

up by the heat.___ You get up to get out at your next stop, but they

push you back down in your seat.___ Your heart____ starts beat-in' fast-er as you

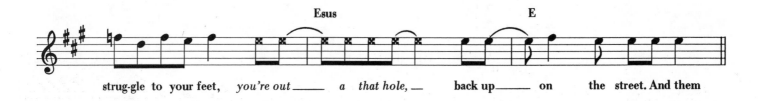

strug-gle to your feet, *you're out____ a that hole,___* back up____ on the street. And them

South Side sis-ters sure look pret-ty, the crip-pled on the cor-ner cries out,

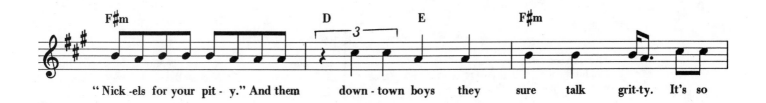

"Nick-els for your pit-y." And them down-town boys they sure talk grit-ty. It's so

hard to be a saint in the Cit-y.___

JACKSON CAGE

Words and Music by
BRUCE SPRINGSTEEN

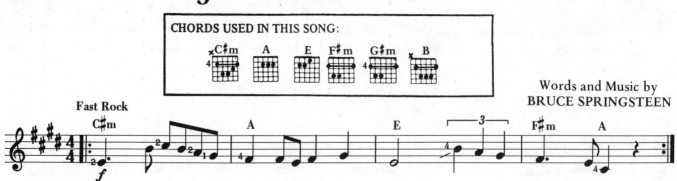

CHORDS USED IN THIS SONG:

Driv-ing home she grabs some-thing to eat, turns a cor-ner and
Ev -ery day ends in wast -ed mo -tion, just crossed swords on the
Baby, there's nights when I dream of a better world, but I wake up so

drives down her street. In -to a row of hous -es she just melts a -way
kill -ing floor. To set -tle back is to settle with -out know -ing
down -hearted, girl. I see you feel -ing so tired and con -fused.

like the sce -n'ry in an -oth -er man's play, in -to a house where the
the hard edge that you're set -tling for. Be -cause there's al -ways just
I won -der what it's worth to me or you. Just wait -ing to

blinds are closed to keep from see-ing things she don't want to know.
one more day, and it's al -ways gon -na be that way.
see more sun, nev -er know-ing if that day will ev -er come.

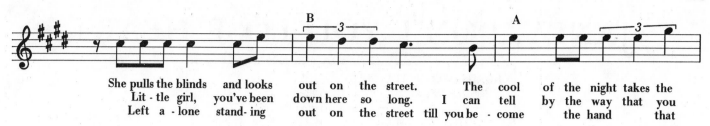

She pulls the blinds and looks out on the street. The cool of the night takes the
Lit - tle girl, you've been down here so long. I can tell by the way that you
Left a - lone stand- ing out on the street till you be - come the hand that

edge off the heat in the ⎫
move you be - long to the ⎬ Jack - son Cage,   down — in the
turns the key down in ⎭

Jack - son Cage.___   You can try   with
                                                       And it don't matter   just
                                                       Well, dar -lin', can   you

all   your might,   but you're re -mind - ed ev - ery night____
what   you say. Are you   tough e -nough to play   the game   they play,or will you
un - der -stand the   way   that they   will turn   a man___into a

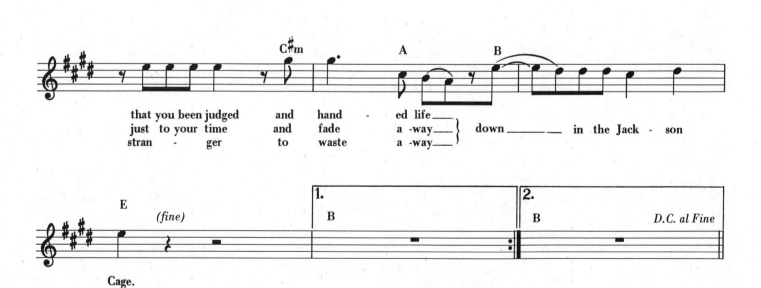

that you been judged   and   hand - ed life___ ⎫
just to your time   and   fade   a -way___ ⎬ down_____ in the Jack - son
stran - ger   to   waste   a -way___ ⎭

1. B   **2.** B   *D.C. al Fine*

E *(fine)*

Cage.

JANEY, DON'T YOU LOSE HEART

Words and Music by
BRUCE SPRINGSTEEN

You got   your book,___
Well, you   say you___

___ ba - by, with all ___ your   fears.
___ got   no   new dreams ___ to   touch.

Let me,   hon - ey   and ___ I'll   catch ___ your   tears.
You feel   like ___ a stranger babe ― who   knows ___ too   much. ―

No, no, no, no,   no.   I'll   take ___ your   sor - row if you
You   come ___ home   late ___ and

want me to. —
get un-dressed.

No, no, no, no, no.

Yeah, come
You lie

— to-mor-row that's what I'll do. —
— in bed and feel this emp-ti-ness. —

List-ten to me:

Chorus:

Jan-ey, don't you lose — heart, no, no, no, no. Jan-ey, don't you lose —

— heart, no, no, no, no. Jan-ey, don't you lose — heart, no, no, no, no.

1.2.   D.S. 𝄋   3.4. *etc.*   *Repeat and fade*

Jan-ey don't you lose — heart. —   — heart, no, no, no, no.

Verse 3:
Till every river it runs dry;
Until the sun's torn from the sky;
Till every fear you've felt burst free,
Gone tumblin' down into the sea.
Listen to me...

(To Chorus:)

JEANNIE NEEDS A SHOOTER

CHORDS USED IN THIS SONG:

E or E   A or A   B or B   F#m7   Esus

Moderate Rock

Words and Music by
BRUCE SPRINGSTEEN and
WARREN ZEVON

born down by the riv-er,   where the   dir-ty wa-ter flows.___   And the
She came down from Knights-town, with her hands hard from the line.___   From the

cold   wind cut through me,   it   cut right through my clothes.___ And the
first time I laid eyes on her I knew that she'd be mine.___ Her

an - ger and the yearn - ing   like fe - ver in my veins,___
fa - ther was a law - man,   he swore he'd shoot me dead.___ 'Cause he

set the fire burn-ing.

knew I want-ed Jean-nie, and I'd have her like I said.

Chorus:

Jean-nie needs a shoot-er,   shoot-er like me.   Jean-nie needs a shoot-er.

Jean - nie needs a shoot - er,   shoot -er on her side.

Jean - nie needs a shoot - er.

Jean-nie needs a shoot - er.

The

Verse 3:
We met down by the river
On the final day in May.
And when I leaned down to kiss her,
She did not turn away.
I drew out all my money
And together we did vow,
To meet that very evening
And to get away somehow.

(Chorus:)

Verse 4:
The night was cold and rainy
Down by the borderline.
I was riding hard to meet her
When a shot rang out behind.
As I lay there in the darkness
With a pistol by my side,
Jeannie and her father
Rode off into the night.
Jeannie needs a shooter.

JOHNNY BYE BYE

CHORDS USED IN THIS SONG:

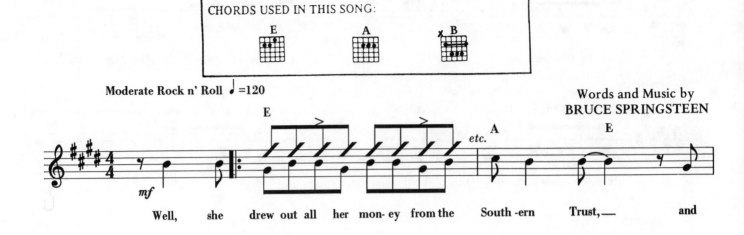

Moderate Rock n' Roll ♩ =120

Words and Music by
BRUCE SPRINGSTEEN

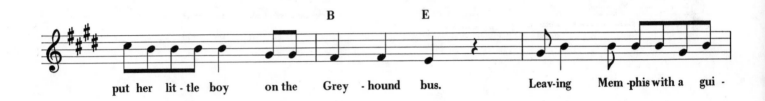

Well, she drew out all her mon-ey from the South-ern Trust, ___ and

put her lit-tle boy on the Grey-hound bus. Leav-ing Mem-phis with a gui-

tar in his hand, ___ on a one way tick-et to the prom-ised land. Well,

hey lit-tle girl ___ with the red dress on, ___ there's a par-ty to-night down in

Mem-phis ___ town. I'll be go-ing down ___ there if you need a ride. ___ A man ___

on the ra - di - o says ___ El - vis Pres - ly died.

(simile)

He drove

Verse 2:
He drove down into Memphis;
The sky was hard and black.
Up over the ridge
Came a white Cadillac.
They drew out all his money,
And they laid him in the back.
A woman cried from the roadside,
"Ah, he's gone, he's gone."
They found him slumped
Up against the drain
With a whole lot of trouble,
Yeah, running through his veins.
Bye, bye Johnny; Johnny, bye bye.
You didn't have to die, you didn't have to die.

JOHNNY 99

Words and Music by
BRUCE SPRINGSTEEN

Verse 2:
Down in the part of town where when you hit a red light you don't stop,
Johnny's wavin' his gun around and threatenin' to blow his top,
When an off-duty cop snuck up on him from behind.
Out in front of the Club Tip Top, they slapped the cuffs on Johnny 99.

Verse 3:
"Now, judge, judge, I got debts no honest man could pay.
The bank was holdin' my mortgage and they was takin' my house away.
Now, I ain't sayin' that makes me an innocent man,
But it was more 'n all this that put that gun in my hand."

Verse 4:
Well, Your Honor, I do believe I'd be better off dead.
And if you can take a man's life for the thoughts that's in his head,
Then won't you sit back in that chair and think it over, judge, one more time,
And let 'em shave off my hair and put me on that execution line."

JUNGLELAND

CHORDS USED IN THIS SONG:

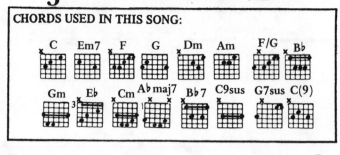

Words and Music by
BRUCE SPRINGSTEEN

Bright ♩=132

fingerpicking

The Rang - ers had __ a home-com - ing in

Har - lem late __ last night, and the Mag -ic Rat drove his sleek ma -

chine o - ver the Jer -sey state line. __

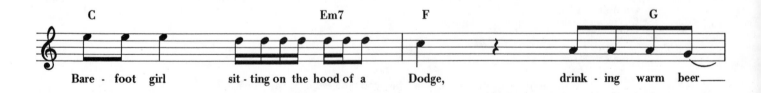

Bare - foot girl sit -ting on the hood of a Dodge, drink -ing warm beer __

__ in the soft __ sum -mer rain. __ The Rat pulls in -to town, rolls up his pants,

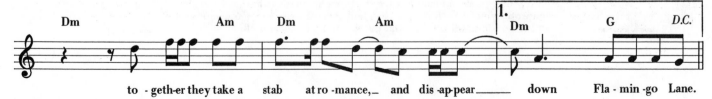

to - geth-er they take a stab at ro -mance, __ and dis -ap-pear __ down Fla - min -go Lane.

2. Jun - gle - land. night. The

street's a - live___ as se - cret debts are paid,___ con - tacts made, they van - ish un -

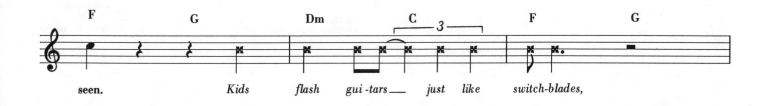

seen. *Kids flash gui -tars___ just like switch-blades,*

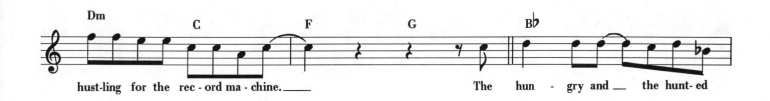

hust-ling for the rec -ord ma - chine.___ The hun - gry and ___ the hunt- ed

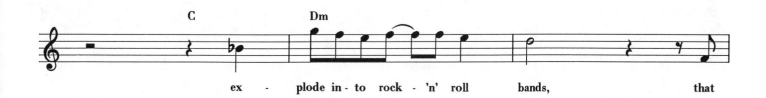

ex - plode in -to rock - 'n' roll bands, that

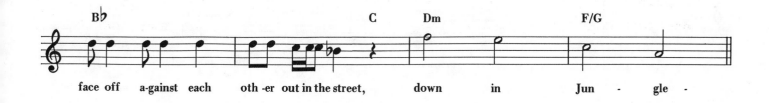

face off a-gainst each oth -er out in the street, down in Jun - gle -

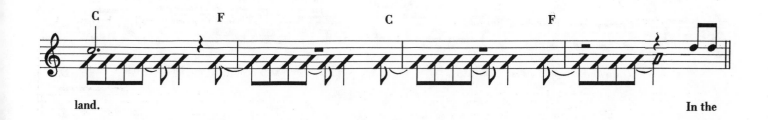

land. In the

112

or as the girl shuts out the bed-room light. Out-side the

street's on fire in a real death waltz, be-tween what's flesh and what's fan - ta - sy. ___

___ And the po-ets down here don't write noth-ing at all, ___ they just

stand back and let it all be. And in the quick of the night, *they reach for their mo-ment and*

try to make an hon-est stand, *but they wind up wound-ed* *not e-ven dead.* To-

night in Jun - gle - land!

Verse 2:
Well, the Maximum Lawmen run down Flamingo,
Chasing the Rat and the barefoot girl.
And the kids round here just like shadows,
Always quiet, holding hands.
From the churches to the jails,
Tonight all is silence in the world,
As we take our stand
Down in Jungleland.

Verse 3:
The midnight gang's assembled
And picked a rendezvous for the night,
They'll meet 'neath that giant Exxon sign
That brings this fair city light.
Man, there's an opera out on the Turnpike,
There's ballet being fought out in the alley,
Until the local cops, Cherry Top,
Rip this holy night.

KITTY'S BACK

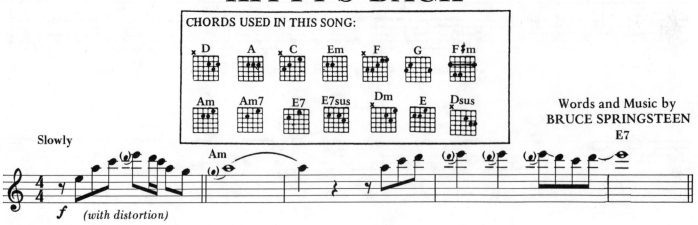

CHORDS USED IN THIS SONG:

Words and Music by
BRUCE SPRINGSTEEN

Slowly

f *(with distortion)*

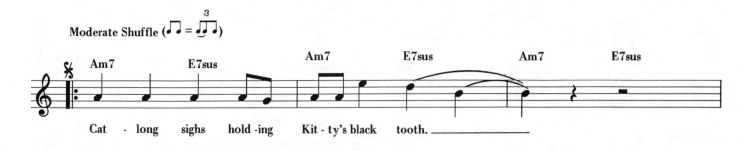

Moderate Shuffle

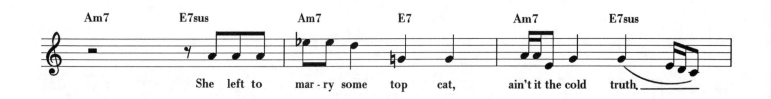

Cat - long sighs hold -ing Kit - ty's black tooth. ____

She left to mar - ry some top cat, ain't it the cold truth. ____

Slightly Faster

And there has - n't been a tal - ly since

Sal - ley left the al - ley, since Kit - ty left with big pret - ty, things have got

pret - ty thin, ____ Oh yeah, it's

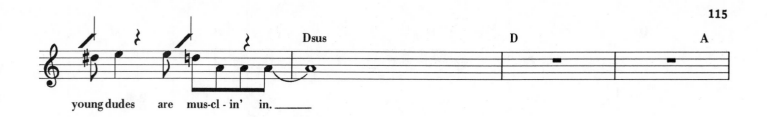

young dudes   are   mus-cl - in'   in. ____

Ooh, ____   what can I   do? ____

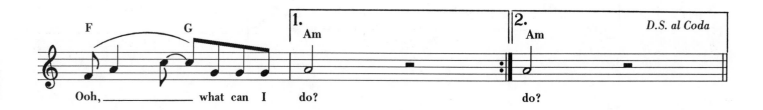

Ooh, _____ what can I   do?   do?

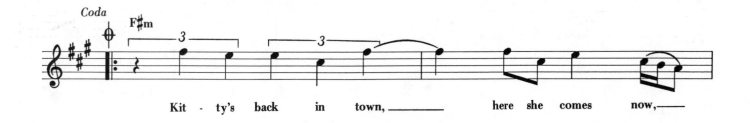

Kit - ty's   back   in   town, _____   here she comes   now, ____

kit - ty's   back   in   town.   town.   Now

Cat knows his Kit - ty's   been un - true, _____

and that she left for a cit - y dude.

Well, she's so soft,___ she's so blue,___

when he looks in - to her eyes,___ he

just sits back__ and sighs:_____ " Ooh,___ what can I

Repeat ad lib and fade

do?___ Ooh,_____ what can I do?"

Verse 2:
Jack knife cries ah,
She goes running nightly through the jungle.
And them tin cans are explodin' out of the ninety degree heat,
Cat somehow lost his baby down on Bleeker Street.
It's sad, but it sure is true.
Cat shrugs his shoulders, sits back and sighs:

Verse 3:
Cat-long lies back bent on a trash can,
Flashing lights, 'cause he's a big wheel
Well, you better learn to move fast when you're young
Or you're not long around,
Cat somehow lost his kitty down in the city pound.
So get right, get tight, get down!
Well, who's that down at the end of the alley?
She's been gone so long.

LOST IN THE FLOOD

Words and Music by
BRUCE SPRINGSTEEN

Verse 2:
That pure American brother, dull-eyed and empty-faced
Races Sundays in a Chevy stock super eight.
He rides'er low on the hip, on the side he's got
  Bound For Glory
In red, white and blue flash paint.
He leans on the hood telling racing stories;
The kids call him Jimmy The Saint.
Well that blaze and noise boy,
He's gunnin' that bitch loaded to blastin' point.
He rides headfirst into a hurricane and disappears into a point,
And there's nothin' left but some blood where the body fell;
That is, nothin' left that you could sell,
Just junk all across the horizon, a real highwayman's farewell.

Chorus 2:
And I said, "Hey kid, you think that's oil?
Man, that ain't oil that's blood."
I wonder what he was thinking when he hit that storm,
Or was he just lost in the flood?

Verse 3:
Eighth Avenue sailors in satin shirts whisper in the air,
Some storefront incarnation of Maria, she's puttin' on me the stare.
And Bronx's best apostle stand with his hand on his own hardware.
Everything stops, you hear five quick shots, the cops come
  up for air;
And now the whiz-bang gang from uptown, they're shootin'
  up the street.
And that cat from the Bronx starts lettin' loose, but he gets blown
  right off his feet.
And some kid comes blastin' round the corner, but a cop puts
  him right away.
He lays on the street holding his leg screaming something in Spanish,
Still breathing when I walked away.

Chorus 3:
And somebody said, "Hey man, did you see that?
His body hit the street with such a beautiful thud."
I wonder what the dude was sayin'
Or was he just lost in the flood?

Chorus 4:
Hey man, did you see that?
Those poor cats are sure messed up.
I wonder what they were gettin' into,
Or were they just lost in the flood?

MANSION ON THE HILL

Words and Music by
BRUCE SPRINGSTEEN

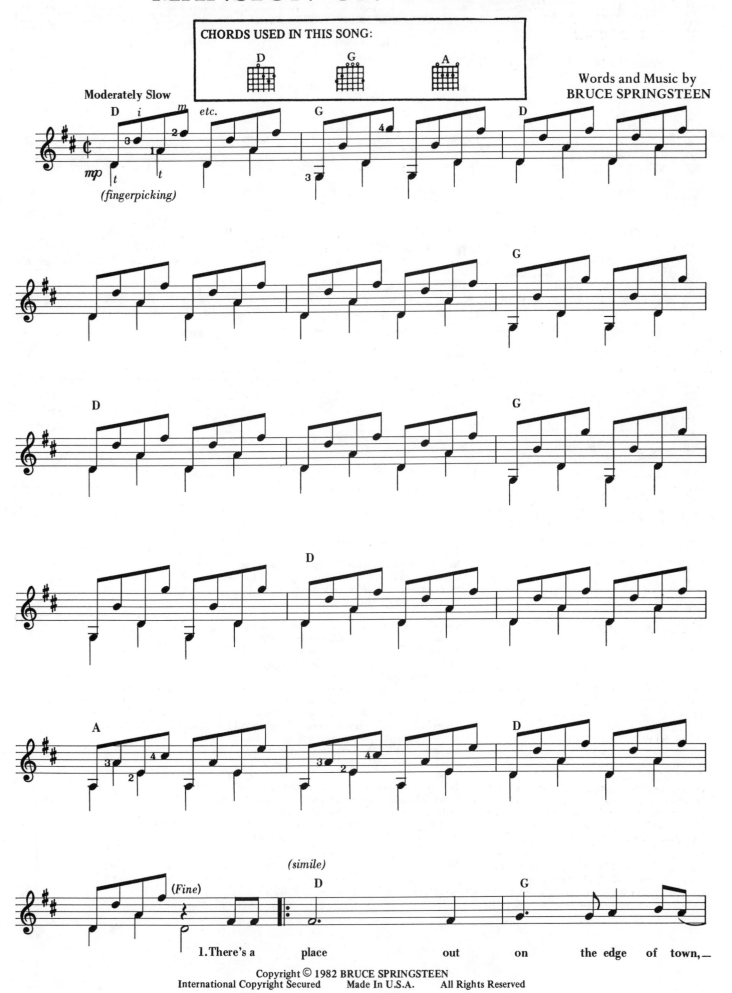

1. There's a place out on the edge of town,—

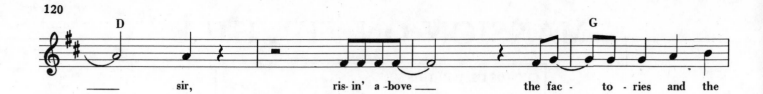

sir, ris- in' a -bove ___ the fac - to - ries and the

fields. Now, ev - er since I was a

child, I can re -mem - ber ___ that man - sion on ___

___ the ___ hill. 2. In the

Verse 2:
In the day you can see the children playing
On the road that leads to those gates of hardened steel.
Steel gates that completely surround, sir,
The mansion on the hill.

Verse 3:
At night my daddy'd take me and we'd ride
Through the streets of a town so silent and still.
Park on a back road along the highway side,
Look up at that mansion on the hill.

Verse 4:
In the summer all the lights would shine.
There'd be music playin', people laughin' all the time.
Me and my sister, we'd hide out in the tall cornfields,
Sit and listen to the mansion on the hill.

Verse 5:
Tonight down here in Linden Town,
I watch the cars rushin' by, home from the mill.
There's a beautiful full moon rising
Above the mansion on the hill.

MARY QUEEN OF ARKANSAS

Words and Music by
BRUCE SPRINGSTEEN

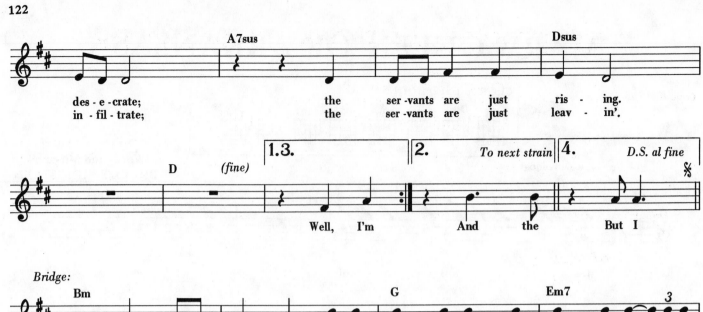

des - e -crate; the ser -vants are just ris - ing.
in - fil - trate; the ser -vants are just leav - in'.

1.3. 2. To next strain 4. D.S. al fine

D (fine)

Well, I'm And the But I

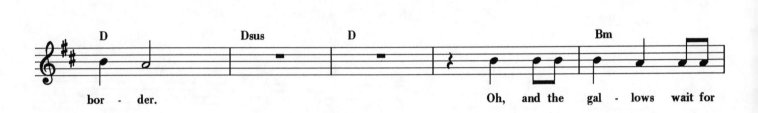

Bridge:

Bm G Em7 3

big top is for dream -ers. We can take the cir - cus all the way — to the

D Dsus D Bm

bor - der. Oh, and the gal - lows wait for

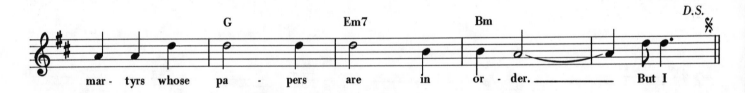

G Em7 Bm D.S.

mar - tyrs whose pa - pers are in or - der. _____ But I

Verse 2:
Well, I'm just a lonely acrobat;
The live wire is my trade.
I've been a shine boy for your acid brat
And a wharf rat of your state.
Mary, my queen, your blows
For freedom are missing.
You're not man enough for me to hate
Or woman enough for kissing.

(To Bridge:)

Verse 3:
Mary queen of Arkansas,
Your white skin is deceivin'.
You wake and wait to lie in bait
And you almost got me believin'.
But on your bed, Mary, I can see
The shadow of a noose.
I don't understand how you can hold me so tight
And love me so damn loose.

Verse 4:
But I know a place where we can go, Mary;
Where I can get a good job
And start all over again clean.
I got contacts deep in Mexico
Where the servants have been seen.

MEETING ACROSS THE RIVER

Words and Music by
BRUCE SPRINGSTEEN

Capo lst fret

Moderately ♩ =96

mf fingerpicking

Hey, Ed-die, can you lend me a few bucks, to - night, can you get us a ride?_ Got-ta make it through_the tun -nel, got a meet-ing with a man __ on the oth - er side. _____ Hey Ed-die ,this guy he's ____ the real ____ thing, ____ so if you want to come a -long, you got -ta prom - ise you won't say an -y-

thing,   'Cause this guy don't dance, ____

and the world's been passed, this is our ____ last   chance.

2. We got-ta
3. Well, Cher-ry

Verse 2:
We gotta stay cool tonight, Eddie,
'Cause man, we got ourselves out on that line.
And if we blow this one,
They ain't gonna be looking for just me this time.
And all we gotta do is hold up our end,
Here, stuff this in your pocket,
It'll look like you're carrying a friend.
And remember, just don't smile,
Change your shirt, 'cause tonight we got style.

Verse 3:
Well, Cherry says she's gonna walk
'Cause she found I took the radio and hocked it.
But Eddie, man, she don't understand
That two grand's practic'ly sitting here in my pocket.
And tonight's gonna be everything that I said,
And when I walk through that door,
I'm just gonna throw that money on the bed.
She'll see this time I wasn't just talking,
Then I'm gonna go out walking.
Hey Eddie, can you catch us a ride?

MY FATHER'S HOUSE

Words and Music by
BRUCE SPRINGSTEEN

Moderately Slow, in 2

Last night I

dreamed _____ that I was a child,

out where the pines _____ grow wild _____ and

tall.   I was___ try - ing to

make it home   thru the for   -   est   be -fore the

dark   ness falls.   2. I heard the wind

Verse 2:
I heard the wind rustling through the trees,
And ghostly voices rose from the fields.
I ran with my heart pounding down that broken path
With the devil snappin' at my heels.

Verse 3:
I broke through the trees, and there in the night
My father's house stood shining hard and bright.
The branches and brambles tore my clothes and scratched my arms.
But I ran till I fell, shaking in his arms.

Verse 4:
I awoke and I imagined the hard things that pulled us apart
Will never again, sir, tear us from each other's hearts.
I got dressed, and to that house I did ride.
From out on the road, I could see its windows shining in light.

Verse 5:
I walked up the steps and stood on the porch.
A woman I didn't recognize came and spoke to me through a chained door.
I told her my story, and who I'd come for.
She said, "I'm sorry, son, but no one by that name lives here anymore."

Verse 6:
My father's house shines hard and bright.
It stands like a beacon calling me in the night.
Calling and calling, so cold and alone,
Shining 'cross this dark highway where our sins lie unatoned.

MY HOMETOWN

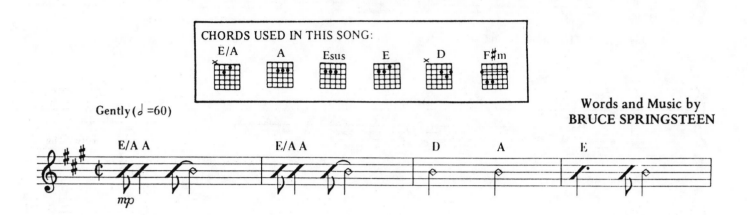

Gently (♩ =60)

Words and Music by
BRUCE SPRINGSTEEN

I was

eight years old ___ and run-ning with ___ a dime in my

hand, in-to the bus stop to pick up a pa-per for

my old ___ man. ___ I'd sit on his lap ___ in that

-y wants to come down here no more. ___ They're

clos-ing down ___ the tex-tile mill ___ a-cross the rail-road tracks.

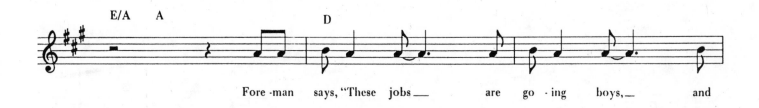

Fore-man says, "These jobs ___ are go-ing boys, ___ and

D.S. al Fine

they ain't com-ing back to

Verse 2:
In sixty-five, tension was running high at my high school,
There was lots of fights between the black and white, there was nothing you could do.
Two cars at a light, on a Saturday night; in a back seat there was a gun.
Words were passed in a shotgun blast, troubled times had come...

Verse 3:
Last night me and Kate, we laid in bed, talking 'bout getting out,
Packing up our bags, maybe heading south.
I'm thirty-five, we got a boy of our own now.
Last night I sat him up, behind the wheel, and said, " Son, take a good look around,
This is your home town."

NEBRASKA

Words and Music by
BRUCE SPRINGSTEEN

1. I saw her stan - din'___ on her front___

lawn, ___ just a twirl - in' ___

her ba - ton. ___ Me and her ___ went ___

for a ride, ___ sir, ___ and ten ___ in -

1.-5.   6.   *D.C. al Fine*

- no-cent peo-ple died. ___   2. From the

Verse 2:
From the town of Lincoln, Nebraska,
With a sawed-off .410 on my lap,
Through to the badlands of Wyoming
I killed everything in my path.

Verse 3:
I can't say that I'm sorry
For the things that we done.
At least for a little while, sir,
Me and her, we had us some fun.

Verse 4:
The jury brought in a guilty verdict,
And the judge, he sentenced me to death.
Midnight in a prison storeroom
With leather straps across my chest.

Verse 5:
Sheriff, when the man pulls that switch, sir,
And snaps my poor head back,
You make sure my pretty baby
Is sittin' right there on my lap.

Verse 6:
They declared me unfit to live.
Said into that great void my soul'd be hurled.
They wanted to know why I did what I did.
Well, sir, I guess there's just a meanness in this world.

NEW YORK CITY SERENADE

Words and Music by
BRUCE SPRINGSTEEN

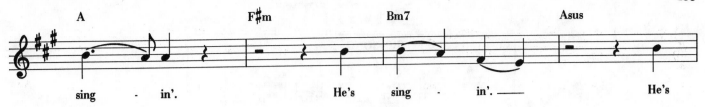

sing - in'. He's sing - in'. ___ He's

sing - in'. All dressed up in sat - in, walk- in' down the

al - ley. He's sing - in', sing - in',

sing - in', ___ sing - in', ___

Verse 2:
Fish lady, oh fish lady,
She baits them tenement walls.
She won't take corner boys,
They ain't got no money
And they're so easy.
I said, "Hey baby, ah, really
Won't you take my hand,
Walk with me down Broadway, yeah.
I'm a young man and talkin' real loud,
Yeah, babe walin' real proud for ya."
Ah, so shake it away,
So shake away your street life,
Shake away your city life
And hook up to the train.
Ah, hook up to the night train.
Hook it up. But I know that she. . .

(To Coda)

NIGHT

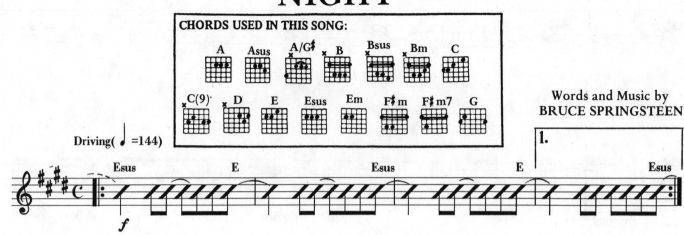

Words and Music by
BRUCE SPRINGSTEEN

Driving (♩ =144)

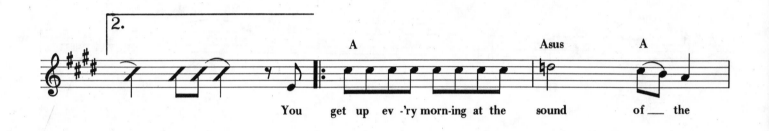

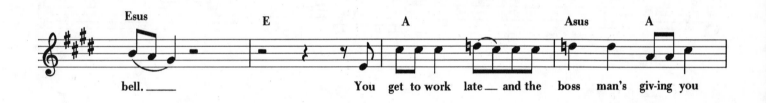

You get up ev-'ry morn-ing at the sound of ___ the

bell. ___ You get to work late ___ and the boss man's giv-ing you

hell. Till you're out ___ on a mid-night run, los-ing your heart ___

___ to a beau-ti-ful one. And it feels right, ___

as you lock up the house, turn out the lights and

step out in-to the night. _____ And the

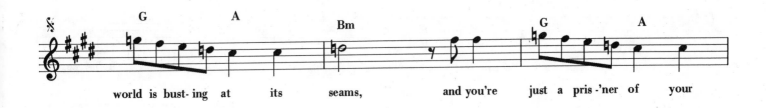

world is bust-ing at its seams, and you're just a pris-'ner of your

dreams, hold-ing on for your life. 'Cause you work all day to blow _____

_____ 'em a-way in the night.

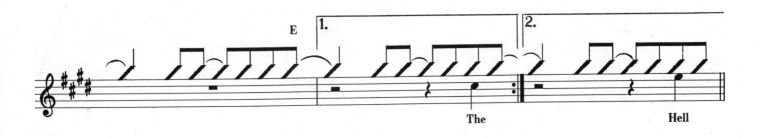

The   Hell

all day they're bust-ing you up on the out-side. _____

to-night you're gon-na break on through to the in-side _____ and it-'ll be right, it-'ll be right and it-'ll be to-night. _____

D.S. al Coda

And you

Coda

night.

You run sad __ and free un-til all you can see is the night!

Additional lyrics:
The rat traps filled with soul crusaders.
The circuits lined and jammed with chromed invaders.
And she's so pretty your lost in the stars,
As you jockey your way through the cars,
And sit at the light, as it changes to green.
With your faith in your machine,
Off you scream into the night.

And you're in love with all the wonder it brings,
And every muscle in your body sings, as the highway ignites.
You work nine to five, and somehow you survive till the night.

And you know she'll be waiting there,
And you'll find her somehow you swear, somewhere tonight.
You run sad and free until all you can see is the night!

NO SURRENDER

to pound. You say you've tired and you just want to

close your eyes and fol-low your dreams down. Well, we

Chorus:

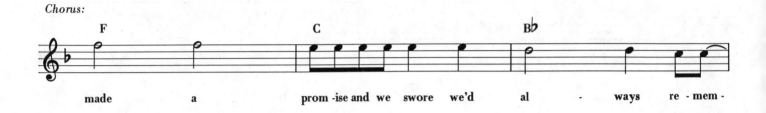

made a prom-ise and we swore we'd al - ways re - mem-

ber. No re - treat, ba - by, no sur -

ren - der. __
{ 1.Like sol - diers in __ the
{ 2.3.Blood bro - thers in __ the

win-ter's night, __ } with a vow __ to de -fend, __ no re -
storm-y night, __ }

1.   D.S. %

treat, ba - by, no sur - ren - der. __   2.Well, now

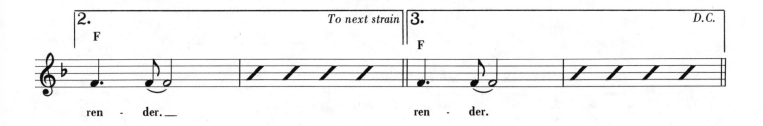

ren - der.___

ren - der.

Lay, lay___ lay, lay, ___ lay, lay, ___ lay, lay, lay, lay, ___ lay,

lay.

Lay, lay, ___ lay, lay, ___ lay, lay, ___ lay,

lay, lay, lay, ___ lay, lay.

3. Now,

Verse 2:
Well, now young faces grow sad and old and hearts of fire grow cold.
We swore blood brothers against the wind. I'm ready to grow young again,
And hear your sister's voice calling us home across the open yards.
Well, maybe we'll cut some place of our own with these drums and these guitars.

Verse 3:
Now, on the street tonight the lights grow dim; the walls of my room are closing in.
There's a war outside still raging; you say it ain't ours anymore to win.
I want to sleep beneath peaceful skies in my lover's bed,
With a wide open country in my eyes and these romantic dreams in my head.

OPEN ALL NIGHT

CHORDS USED IN THIS SONG:

Words and Music by
BRUCE SPRINGSTEEN

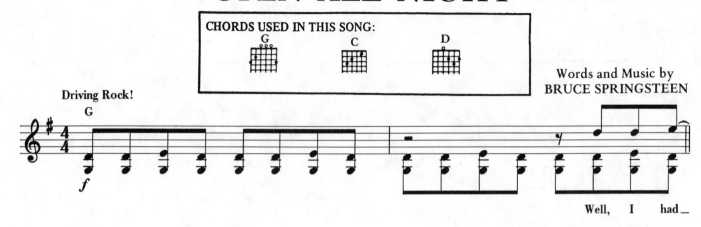

Driving Rock!

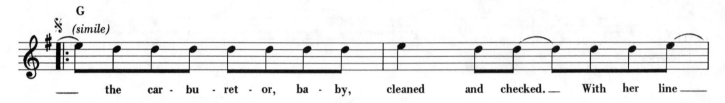

Well, I had

___ the car - bu - ret - or, ba - by, cleaned and checked. ___ With her line ___

___ blown out she's hum - min' like a tur - bo - jet. ___ Propped her up ___

___ in the back ___ yard on con - crete blocks ___ for a new ___

___ clutch plate and a new set of shocks. ___ Took her down ___

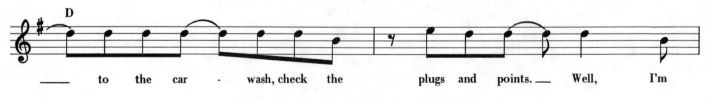

___ to the car - wash, check the plugs and points. ___ Well, I'm

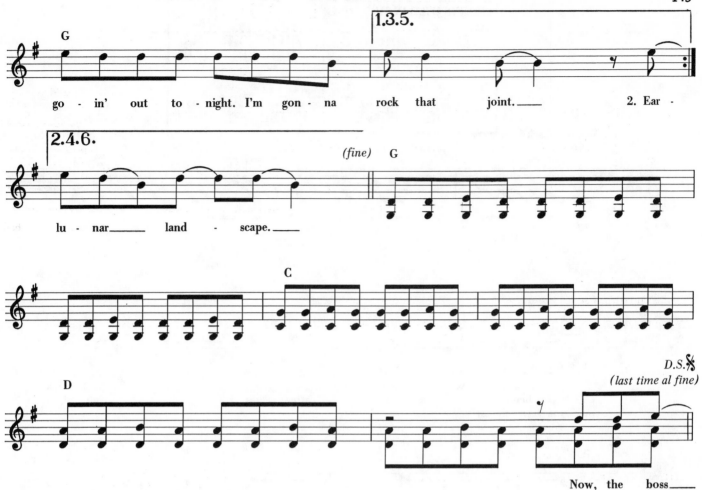

1.3.5.

go - in' out to - night. I'm gon - na rock that joint.____ 2. Ear -

2.4.6.

(fine) G

lu - nar____ land - scape.____

C

D

D.S. 𝄋
(last time al fine)

Now, the boss____

Verse 2:
Early north Jersey industrial skyline,
I'm a all-set cobra jet creepin' through the nighttime.
Gotta find a gas station; gotta find a pay phone.
This turnpike sure is spooky at night when you're all alone.
Gotta hit the gas, baby. I'm runnin' late.
This New Jersey in the mornin' like a lunar landscape.

Verse 3:
Now, the boss don't dig me, so he put me on the night shift.
It's an all-night run to get back to where my baby lives.
In the wee, wee hours your mind gets hazy.
Radio relay towers, won't you lead me to my baby?
Underneath the overpass, trooper hits his party light switch.
Good night, good luck. One, two power shift.

Verse 4:
I met Wanda when she was employed
Behind the counter at Route Sixty Bob's Big Boy Fried Chicken.
On the front seat, she's sittin' in my lap.
We're wipin' our fingers on a Texaco road map.
I remember Wanda up on scrap metal hill
With them big brown eyes that make your heart stand still.

Verse 5:
Well, at five a.m., oil pressure's sinkin' fast.
I make a pit stop, wipe the windshield, check the gas.
Gotta call my baby on the telephone,
Let her know that her daddy's comin' on home.
Sit tight, little mama, I'm comin' 'round.
I got three more hours, but I'm coverin' ground.

Verse 6:
Your eyes get itchy in the wee, wee hours.
Sun's just a red ball risin' over them refinery towers.
Radio's jammed up with gospel stations.
Lost souls callin' long distance salvation.
Hey, mister deejay, won'tcha hear my last prayer?
Hey, ho, rock 'n' roll, deliver me from nowhere.

OUT IN THE STREET

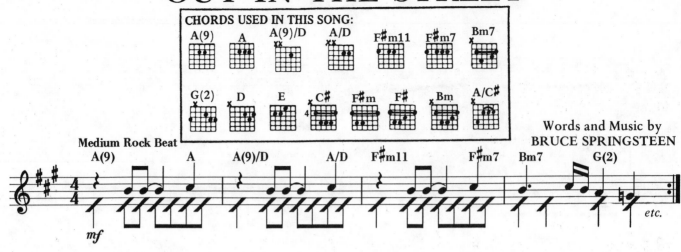

Words and Music by
BRUCE SPRINGSTEEN

Medium Rock Beat

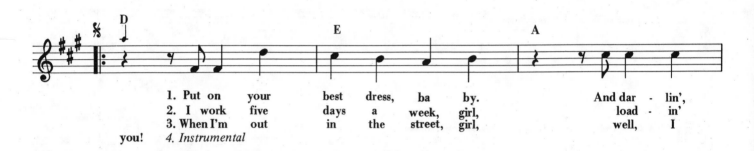

1. Put on your best dress, ba - by. And dar - lin',
2. I work five days a week, girl, load - in'
3. When I'm out in the street, girl, well, I

you! 4. Instrumental

fix your hair up right, 'cause there's a par - ty, hon - ey,
crates down on the dock. I take my hard -earned mon - ey
nev - er feel a - lone. When I'm out in the street, girl,

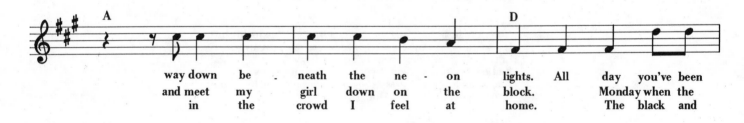

way down be - neath the ne - on lights. All day you've been
and meet my girl down on the block. Monday when the
in the crowd I feel at home. The black and

work -in' that hard line. Now to - night you're gon - na have__ a good
fore - man calls "time", I've al - ready got Fri - day on __ my
whites, they cruise by, and they watch us from the cor - ner of __ their

1.
time.__

2.3.4.

mind. When__ that whis - tle
eye. But__ there ain't no
When__ that whis - tle

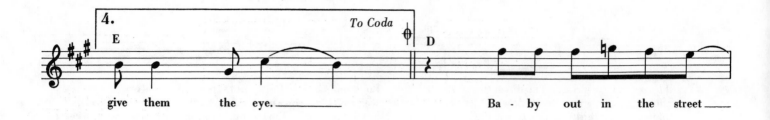

give them the eye.___ Ba - by out in the street___

___ I don't feel sad___ or blue.___

Ba - by, out in the street___ I'll be wait - in' for

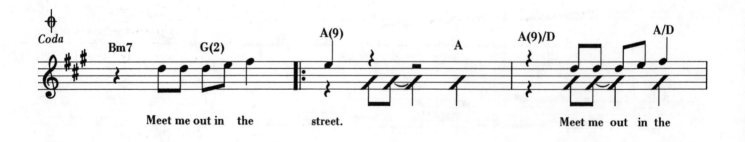

Meet me out in the street. Meet me out in the

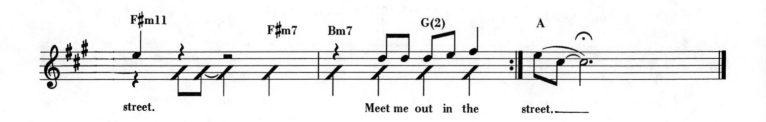

street. Meet me out in the street.___

OUT OF WORK

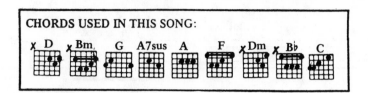

Words and Music by
BRUCE SPRINGSTEEN

Eight A. M. I'm up and my feet beat-in' on the side-walk.
I go to pick my girl up. Her name is Lin-da Brown.

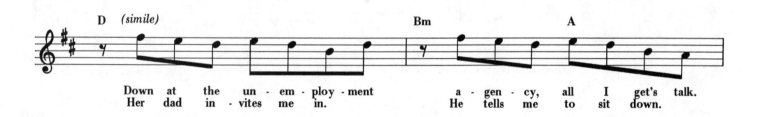

Down at the un-em-ploy-ment a-gen-cy, all I get's talk.
Her dad in-vites me in. He tells me to sit down.

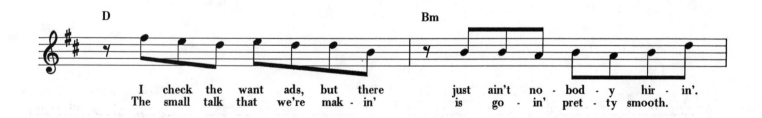

I check the want ads, but there just ain't no-bod-y hir-in'.
The small talk that we're mak-in' is go-in' pret-ty smooth.

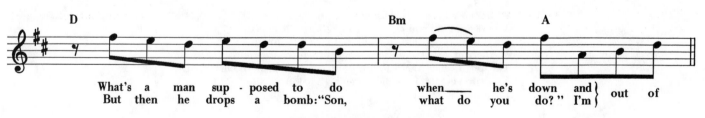

What's a man sup-posed to do when he's down and out of
But then he drops a bomb: "Son, what do you do?" I'm out of

Chorus:

work.

I need a job. I'm out of work.

I'm un-em-ployed. I'm out of work.

I need a job. I'm out of work.

1.

2. To next strain
Yeah, yeah, yeah.—

3. fine

Sax solo adapted for guitar

D.S. al fine

Verse 3:
Hey, Mister President, I know you got good plans.
You're doin' all you can, now, to help the little man.
We got to do our best to whip that inflation down.
Maybe you've got a job for me just drivin' you around.
The tough times, there ain't nothin'. Make a man lose his mind.
Up there you got a job, but doen here below
I'm out of . . .

(To Chorus:)

PINK CADILLAC

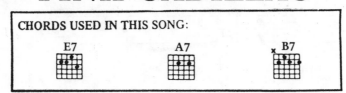

CHORDS USED IN THIS SONG:

Driving blues

Words and Music by
BRUCE SPRINGSTEEN

1. Well, now you __

__ might think I'm fool - in' for the fool - ish things __ I do. __

__ You may won - der how come I love __ you, when you get on __

__ my nerves __ like you do. Well, ba - by, you know you bug __

__ me, there ain't __ no se - cret 'bout that. Well, come on __

__ o - ver here and hug __ me, ba - by, I'll spill the facts. __

Well, hon - ey it ain't __ your mon - ey 'cause ba -by,

I got plen - ty of that. ___ I love you for your

pink Cad -il -lac, crushed __ vel -vet seats, rid - ing in the back, ooz -

- ing down the street, wav - ing to the girls, feel -

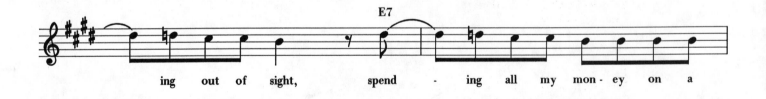

ing out of sight, spend - ing all my mon - ey on a

Sat - ur -day night. Hon - ey I just won - der what {you
{it

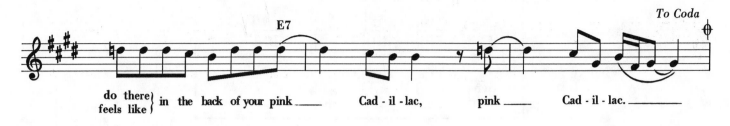

To Coda

do there }
feels like } in the back of your pink ____ Cad - il - lac, pink ____ Cad - il - lac. ____

1.   **2.**

2. Well, now way __

D.S. al Coda

3.Now, some __

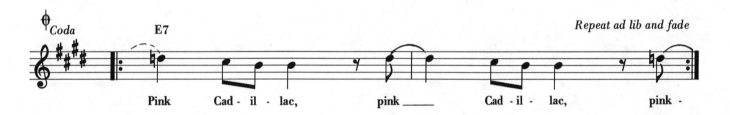

Coda   *Repeat ad lib and fade*

Pink   Cad - il - lac,   pink ____   Cad - il - lac,   pink -

Verse 2:
Well now, way back in the Bible, temptations always come along.
There's always somebody temptin' you, somebody into doin' something they know is wrong.
Well, they tempt you, man, with silver,
And they tempt you, sir, with gold.
And they tempt you with the pleasures that the flesh does surely hold.
They say Eve tempted Adam with an apple,
But man I ain't goin' for that,
I know it was her ...

(To Chorus:)

Verse 3:
Now, some folks say it's too big, and uses too much gas,
Some folks say it's too old, and that it goes too fast.
But my love is bigger than a Honda, it's bigger than a Subaru.
Hey, man, there's only one thing, and one car that'll do.
Anyway, we don't have to drive it, honey we can park it out in back,
And have a party in your ...

(To Chorus:)

POINT BLANK

Words and Music by
BRUCE SPRINGSTEEN

Do you still

say your prayers____ lit - tle dar - lin'? Do you go to bed____ at night
up where young____ girls, they grow up fast. You took what you were hand-ed and left be-

hind what was asked. pray - in' that____ to - mor - row ev - ery-
But what they asked, ba - by, wasn't right.

thing will be all____ right? But to - mor - rows fall____ in num-
You didn't have to live that life. And I was gonna be your Ro - me - o you were gon-na

ber, in num-ber, one by one. You

be my Juliet. These days, you don't wait on Ro-me-os, you wait on that welfare check

wake up and you're dy - ing. You don't

and on all the pretty little things that you can't ever have,

1.2.4. *To next strain* **3.**

e - ven know what from. Well, they shot you on the floor. 4. You just stood there

all the prom - is - es that al-ways end up

Chorus:

point blank. You been shot in the back.

point blank. Shot be-tween the eyes,

Ba - by, point blank. You been

oh, point blank, like

fooled this time, lit - tle girl. That's a fact.

little white lies you tell to ease the pain.

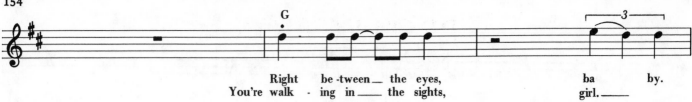

Right be-tween— the eyes, ba by.
You're walk - ing in — the sights, girl.—

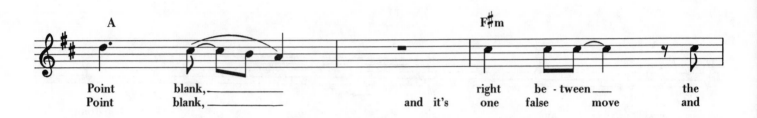

Point blank,_____ right be - tween— the
Point blank,_____ and it's one false move and

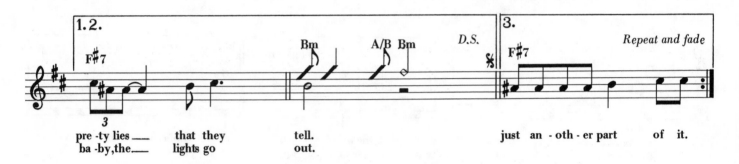

pre -ty lies __ that they tell. just an -oth - er part of it.
ba -by, the__ lights go out.

Verse 3:
Once I dreamed we were together again, baby you and me,
Back home in those old clubs, the way we used to be.
We were standin' at the bar, and it was hard to hear.
The band was playin' loud, and you were shoutin' something in my ear.
You pulled my jacket off, and as the drummer counted four,
You grabbed my hand and pulled me out on the floor.

Verse 4:
You just stood there and held me, and you started dancin' slow.
And as I pulled you tighter, I swore I'd never let you go.
Well, I saw you last night down on the avenue.
Your face was in the shadows, but I knew that it was you.
You were standin' in the doorway, out of the rain.
You didn't answer when I called out your name.
You just turned and then you looked away,
Like just another stranger, waitin' to get blown away.

Chorus:
Point blank, right between the eyes.
Oh, point blank, right between the pretty eyes, you fell.
Point blank, you been shot straight through the heart.
Yeah, point blank
You've been twisted up till you've become just another part of it.

(Repeat Chorus, ad lib and fade)

PROTECTION

CHORDS USED IN THIS SONG:

Words and Music by
BRUCE SPRINGSTEEN

Night af-ter night I keep hold-in' on.
I wait at home by my tel-e-phone,

You say you love me when you leave me so lone-ly.
when I call your house, ba-by, you're not at home.

I don't be-lieve a sin-gle
Knock on the door and I

thing you're say-in';
rush down the stairs.

I think it's all some e-vil
When I op-en up, ba-by,

game you're play-in'.
you're not there.

Still all day long, all I
When we're to-geth-er and you

do is think a-bout ya.
put your arms a-round me,

You got me be-liev-in' that
your love seems a-ware of the con-

PROVE IT ALL NIGHT

Words and Music by
BRUCE SPRINGSTEEN

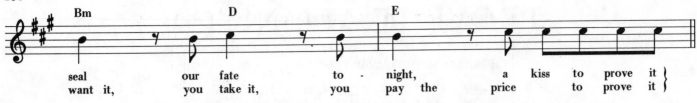

seal   our fate   to - night,   a kiss to prove it
want it,   you take it,   you pay the   price   to prove it

Chorus:

all   night,   prove it all _____ night,   girl there's noth-ing else that we can
(and)

do. _____   So prove it all   night,   prove it all _____ night and girl I'll

prove it all _____ night for   you. _____   Ev - ery

Verse 3:
Baby tie your hair back in a long white bow,
Meet me in the fields behind the dynamo.
You hear voices telling you not to go.
They made their choices and they'll never know
What it means to steal, to cheat, to lie,
What it's like to live and die. Prove it...

(Chorus:)

RACING IN THE STREET

Words and Music by
BRUCE SPRINGSTEEN

(piano part adapted for guitar)

I got a six-ty-nine Chev-y with a
take all the ac-tion we____

three nine-ty-six____ Fuel-ie heads____ and a Hurst on the floor,____ she's
can____ meet____ and we cov-er all the north-east____ states,____ when the

wait-ing to-night____ down in the park-ing lot, out-side the
strip shuts down____ we run 'em in the street, from the

Sev-en E-lev-en store.____ Me and my
fire-roads to the in-ter-state.____ Now

part-ner Son-ny built her straight out of scratch,____ and he rides____
some guys they just give up liv-ing, and start dy-

Verse 3:
I met her on the strip three years ago,
In a Camaro with this dude from L.A.
I blew that Camaro off my back,
And drove that little girl away.
But now there's wrinkles around my baby's eyes
And she cries herself to sleep at night,
When I come home the house is dark,
She sighs, "Baby did you make it all right?"

Verse 4:
She sits on the porch of her daddy's house
But all her pretty dreams are torn,
She stares off alone into the night,
With the eyes of one who hates for just being born.
For all the shut down strangers and hot-rod angels
Rumbling through this promised land,
Tonight my baby and me we're gonna ride to the sea,
And wash these sins off our hands

Chorus:
Tonight, tonight, the highway's bright,
Out of our way mister you best keep,
'Cause summer's here and the time is right
For racing in the street.

RAMROD

CHORDS USED IN THIS SONG:

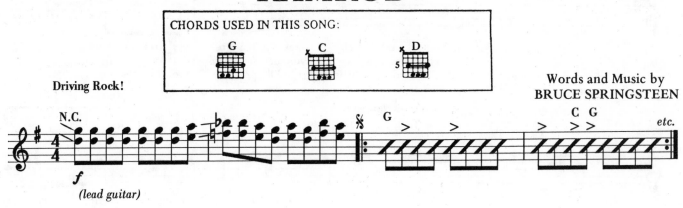

Words and Music by
BRUCE SPRINGSTEEN

Driving Rock!

(lead guitar)

Hey lit - tle dol - ly with the blue jeans on, ___
hot - step - ping hem - i with a four- on- the -floor. ___
Hey lit - tle dol - ly with a say you will. ___

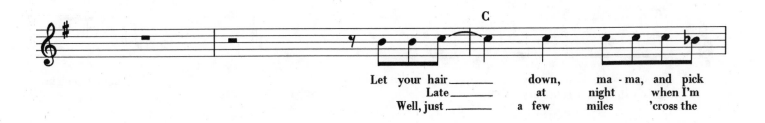

I wan -na ram -rod with you hon- ey, till ___ half past dawn. ___
Well, she's a road - run -ner en - gine in a Thir - ty- two Ford. ___
Meet me to -night ___ up on top of the hill. ___

Let your hair ___ down, ma - ma, and pick
Late ___ at night when I'm
Well, just ___ a few miles 'cross the

up this beat. ___   Come on and
dead on the line, ___   I swear I think of
coun - ty line, ___   well, there's a

meet me to - night down on Blue - bird Street. ___
your pret - ty face when I let her un - wind.
cute lit - tle chapel nes - tled down in the pine.

Copyright © 1980, 1981 BRUCE SPRINGSTEEN
International Copyright Secured   Made In U.S.A.   All Rights Reserved

I've been work-ing all week; I'm up to my neck in hock.___
Well, look o - ver yon -der, see them cit - y___ lights.___
Say you'll be mine, little girl, I'll put my foot to the floor.___

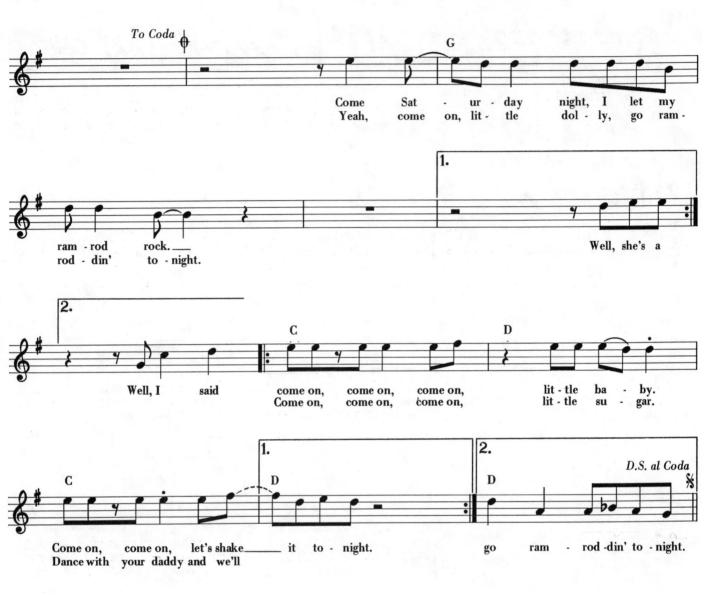

To Coda ⊕

Come Sat - ur - day night, I let my
Yeah, come on, lit - tle dol - ly, go ram -

1.

ram - rod rock.___
rod - din' to - night.

Well, she's a

2.

Well, I said come on, come on, come on, lit - tle ba - by.
Come on, come on, come on, lit - tle su - gar.

1.
2.
D.S. al Coda 𝄋

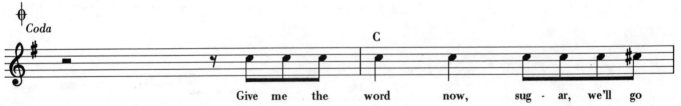

Come on, come on, let's shake___ it to - night.   go ram - rod -din' to - night.
Dance with your daddy and we'll

⊕ *Coda*

Give me the word now, sug - ar, we'll go

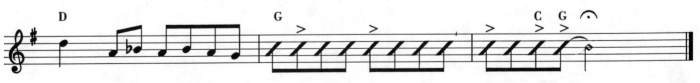

ram - rod -din' for - ev - er more.

REASON TO BELIEVE

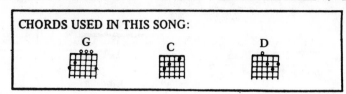

Words and Music by
BRUCE SPRINGSTEEN

Moderate Shuffle

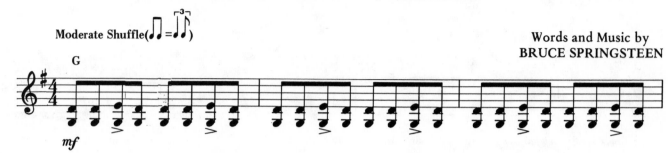

Seen a man stand-in' o-ver a   dead ____ dog   by the high- way in a

ditch.   He's look-in' down kind -a puz - zled,

pok-in' that .dog with a stick. ___   Got his car   door   flung

o - pen. He's   stand-in' out on High - way Thir -ty - one,

like if he stood there long   e - nough,   that dog'd get up and

run.   It struck me kind-a fun - ny.

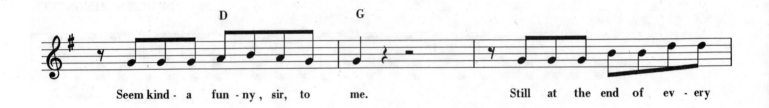

Seem kind - a fun - ny, sir, to   me.   Still at the end of ev - ery

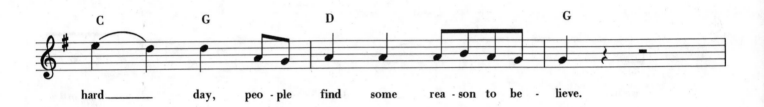

hard_____ day,   peo - ple find   some   rea - son to be - lieve.

2. Now, Mar - y   Lou   loved

Verse 2:
Now, Mary Lou loved Johnny with a love mean and true.
She said, "Baby, I'll work for you every day and bring my money home to you."
One day he up and left her, and ever since that,
She waits down at the end of that dirt road for young Johnny to come back.
It struck me kind-a funny, funny, yeah, indeed,
How at the end of every hard-earned day, people find some reason to believe.

Verse 3:
Take a baby to the river. Kyle William they called him.
Wash the baby in the water. Take away little Kyle's sin.
In a whitewash shotgun shack an old man passes away.
Take the body to the graveyard. Over him they pray.
Lord, won't you tell us, tell us, what does it mean?
At the end of every hard-earned day, people find some reason to believe.

Verse 4:
Congregation gathers down by the riverside.
Preacher stands with a Bible; groom stands waitin' for his bride.
Congregation gone and the sun sets behind a weepin' willow tree.
Groom stands alone and watches the river rush on so effortlessly,
Wonderin' where can his baby be.
Still at the end of every hard-earned day, people find some reason to believe.

RENDEZVOUS

CHORDS USED IN THIS SONG:

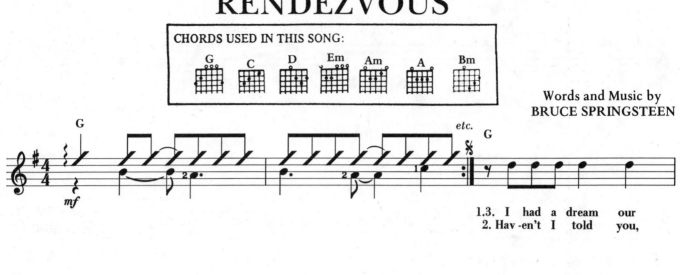

Words and Music by
BRUCE SPRINGSTEEN

1.3. I had a dream our
2. Hav-en't I told you,

love would last for - ev - er,
girl, how much I like you,

I had a dream to -
I got a feel - ing

night my dream comes true.
that you like me too.

And she'll be there to -
And if you'll hold me

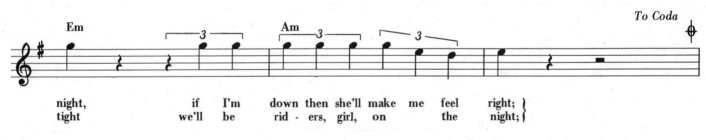

night,   if I'm   down then she'll make me feel   right;
tight   we'll be   rid - ers, girl, on   the   night;

ooh _____ ren - dez - vous.

vous.   We de - serve

so   much more than this,   girl.   We're

rid - ing   on   the pow - er   and   liv - ing on   the prom - ise   in

D.S. al Coda   *Coda*

your   last   kiss.   Be - cause   I   ooh, ____

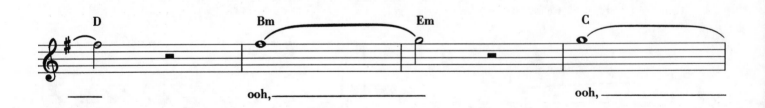

____   ooh, _____   ooh, _____

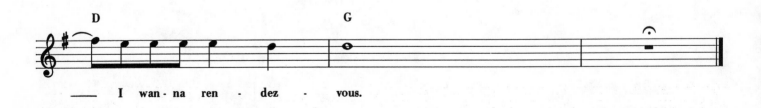

____ I wan - na ren - dez - vous.

ROSALITA
(Come Out Tonight)

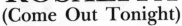

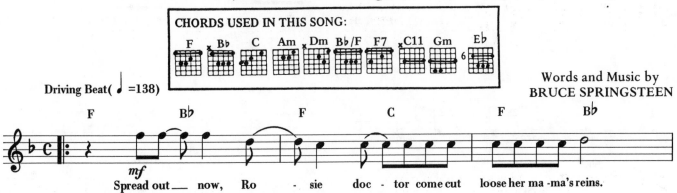

Words and Music by
BRUCE SPRINGSTEEN

Driving Beat (♩ =138)

Spread out___ now, Ro - sie doc - tor come cut loose her ma -ma's reins.

You know play-in' blind - man's bluff ___ is a lit -tle ba -by's game.___

You pick up Lit -tle Dy - na -mite, I'm ___

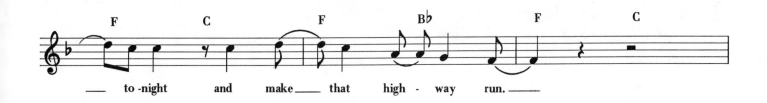

___ gon-na pick up Lit - tle Gun,____ and to - geth -er we're gon - na go out ____

___ to -night and make ___ that high - way run. ___

You don't have to call me lieu - ten -nant Ros - sie, and I don't want to be ___ your son.___

The on-ly lov-er I'm ev-er gon-na need's your soft,

sweet lit-tle girl's tongue, and Ro-sie you're the one.

Ro-sa-li-ta jump a lit-tle light-er. Se-ño-ri-ta come sit by my fire, I just

want to be your lov-er, ain't no li-ar Ro-sa-

li-ta, you're my stone de-sire. -sire.

Now

Verse 2:
Dynamite's in the belfry, baby, playin' with the bats,
Little Gun's downtown in front of Woolworth's tryin' out his attitude on all the cats.
Papa's on the corner waitin' for the bus, Mama, she's home in the window waitin up for us.
She'll be there in that chair when they wrestle her upstairs, 'cause you know we ain't gonna come,
I ain't here on business, baby, I'm only here for fun. And Rosie your the one.

Verse 3:
Jack the Rabbit and Weak Knee Willie, don't you know they're gonna be there,
Ah, Sloppy Sue and Big Bones Billy, they'll be comin' up for air.
We're gonna play some pool, skip some school, act real cool, stay out all night, it's gonna feel alright.
So Rosie come out tonight, little baby, come out tonight.
Windows are for cheaters, chimneys for the poor, oh, closets are for hangers, winners use the door.
So use it, Rosie, that's what it's there for.

Verse 4:
And my tires were slashed and I almost crashed, but the Lord had mercy,
And my machine, she's a dud, out stuck in the mud somewhere in the swamps of New Jersey.
Well, hold on tight, stay up all night, 'cause Rosie, I'm comin' on strong.
By the time we meet in the morning light I will hold you in my arms.
I know a pretty little place in Southern California, down San Diego way.
There's a little café where they play guitars all night and all day,
You can hear them in the back room strumin'
So hold tight, baby, 'cause don't you know daddy's comin'. Ah, everybody sing.

SAVIN' UP

Words and Music by
BRUCE SPRINGSTEEN

Moderate Rock

(bass part adapted for guitar)

(simile)

You may have dia - monds,   you may have pearls.
You may have a big back-yard   and ru - by rings,
You need a strong man, ba - by,   to love and understand

ya;   You may think you got it, ba - by, ov - er
and my love is just a   sec-ond place runner, hon - ey,
a man who ain't   a - fraid, sug - ar,

all the oth - er girls.   But hon- ey you ain't
to your fan - cy things.   But what you got to
to get some dirt on his hands for you.   And when you're feel- in'

got noth - in'   and I'll tell you why.
hold on to   when the lights go down,
so down-heart-ed   and all you want to do is cry,

If you're emp-ty as a soul___ can be,___ ba - by, way___ down in - side;
you come look - in' for me ba - by, but I ain't no-where a - round.__
just come on take my hand ___ ba - by, to - geth - er you and I.___

Chorus:

you bet -ter start
You bet -ter start } sav - in' up for the things___ that mon-
We could start

ey can't buy.___ You bet -ter start sav - in' up

for the things___ that mon - ey can't buy.___ You bet -ter start

sav - in' up for the things___ that mon - ey can't buy.___

You bet -ter start sav - in' up for the things___ that mon-

1. 2.   **3.**

ey can't buy.___

SHE'S THE ONE

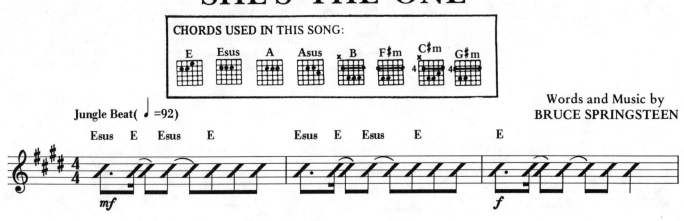

CHORDS USED IN THIS SONG:
E Esus A Asus xB F#m C#m G#m

Words and Music by
BRUCE SPRINGSTEEN

Jungle Beat (♩=92)

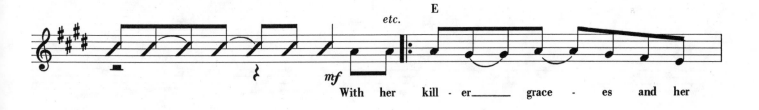

Esus E Esus E   Esus E Esus E   E

mf   *f*

etc.   E

mf

With her kill - er___ grace - es and her

se -cret___ plac - es that no boy can___ fill___   With her

hands on her hips, oh, and that smile on her lips be - cause she

A

knows that it kills me.___   With her soft French___ cream stand-ing in the

door - way like a dream___ I wish she'd just leave me a - lone

Be - cause French cream won't ___ soft - en them boots,

and French ___ kiss - es will not break that heart of stone ___

With her long hair ___ fall - ing and her

eyes that ___ shine like a mid -night sun ___ Oh o, she's the

one. She's the one. With the

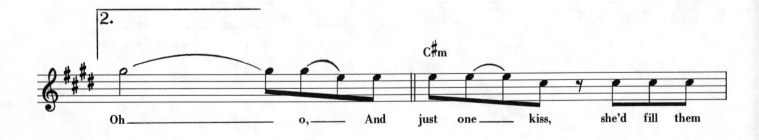

Oh ___ o, ___ And just one ___ kiss, she'd fill them

long sum-mer nights___ with her ten - der - ness.___ The se -cret

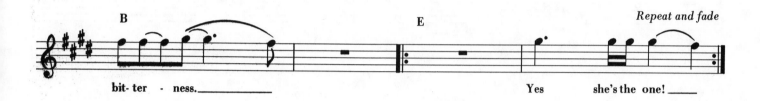

pact you___ made___ back when her love could___ save___ you from the

bit- ter - ness._____ Yes she's the one! _____

Repeat and fade

Additional lyrics:
With the thunder in your heart, at night when you're kneeling in the dark,
It says your never gonna leave her
But there's this angel in her eyes that tells such desp'rate lies,
And all you want to do is believe her.
And tonight you'll try just one more time to leave it all behind,
And break on through.
Oh, she can take you, but if she wants to break you,
She's gonna find out that ain't so easy to do.
And no matter where you sleep tonight, or how far you run
Oh, she's the one.

SHERRY DARLING

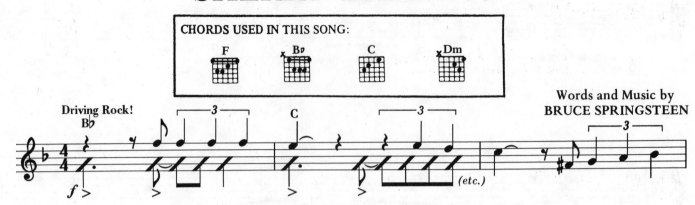

Words and Music by
BRUCE SPRINGSTEEN

Your ma-ma's / yap-pin' in ___ the back seat. / Tell her to push
girls melt - in' ___ on the beach, / and they're so
(3rd time instrumental)

o - ver and move ___ them big feet. / Ev - ery Mon - day morn -
fine but so ___ out of reach, / 'cause I'm

ing I got - ta drive ___ her down ___ to the un - em - ploy - ment a - gen -
stuck in traf - fic down here ___ on Fif - ty - third

cy. / Well, this morn - ing I ain't fight - ing. Tell her I give ___
Street. / Now, Sher - ry, my love for you is ___

up.   Tell her   she   wins   if   she'll   just   shut ___ up.   But it's the
real,   but   I   didn't   count   on   this   pack - age ___ deal.   And, ba - by,

last   time ___ that   she's   gon- na   be   rid - in' with   me. ___
this   car ___ just   ain't   big   e -nough for   her   and   me. ___

Chorus:

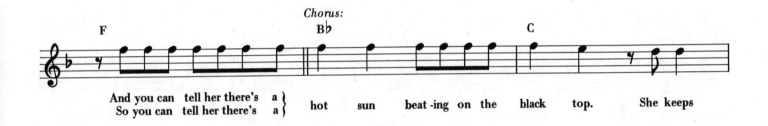

And you can   tell her there's   a   hot   sun   beat -ing on   the   black   top.   She keeps
So you can   tell her there's   a

talk - in', she'll be   walk - in' that last _____ block.   She can   take   a   sub - way   back ___

___ to   the ghet -to to -night. _____   Well, I   got   some

beer,   and the   high - way's   free.   And   I   got   you, and, ba - by, you   got

To Coda

me.   Hey, hey hey,   what do you say,   Sher - ry

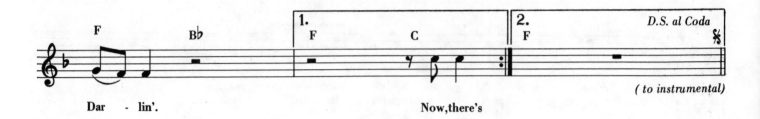

Dar - lin'.   Now, there's

(to instrumental)

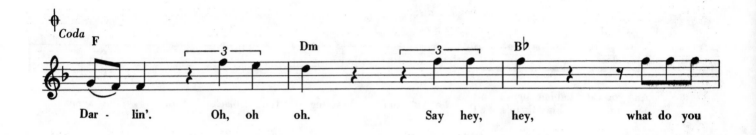

Dar - lin'.   Oh, oh oh.   Say hey, hey,   what do you

say,   Sher - ry Dar - lin'.

Verse 3: Instrumental

Chorus II:
Well, let there be sunlight, let there be rain,
Let the broken-hearted love again.
Sherry, we can run with our arms open wide before the tide.
To all the girls down at Sacred Heart
And all you operators back in the Park,
Say hey, hey, hey, what do you say,
Sherry Darlin'. Oh, oh, oh.
Say hey, hey, what do you say,
Sherry Darlin'.

SHUT OUT THE LIGHT

Words and Music by
BRUCE SPRINGSTEEN

Verse 3:
Well, on his porch he stretched a banner that said, "Johnny welcome home".
Bobby pulled his Ford out of the garage, and they polished up the chrome.
His mama said, "Johnny, oh Johnny, I'm so glad to have you back with me."
His pa said he was sure they'd give him his job back down at the factory.

(To Chorus:)

Verse 4:
Well, deep in the dark forest, forest filled with rain,
Beyond the strip of Maryland pines, there's a river without a name.
In the cold black water where Johnson Linnier stands,
He stares across the lights of the city and dreams of where he's been.

(To Chorus:)

SOMETHING IN THE NIGHT

Words and Music by
BRUCE SPRINGSTEEN

guts,
on } hmm _____ of some-thing in the night. ____

1. You're **2.3.** (Fine) Noth-ing is ___ for - got - ten or ___ for -

giv - en when it's your last time ___ a - round.

I got stuff run - ning round ___ my head that I just can't live

down. _____ When we

Verse 3:
When we found the things we loved,
They were crushed and dying in the dirt,
We tried to pick up the pieces,
And get away without getting hurt.
But they caught us at the state line,
Burned our cars in one last fight,
And left us running burned and blind,
Hmm, chasing something in the night.

SPIRIT IN THE NIGHT

CHORDS USED IN THIS SONG:

Moderate Shuffle

Words and Music by
BRUCE SPRINGSTEEN

Cra - zy Jan - ey and her mis - sion man were
Bil - ly slammed on his coast - er brakes and said, "Anybody would

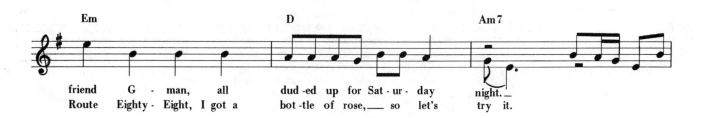

back in the al - ley trad - in' hands.   'Long came Wild Bil - ly with his
wanna go on up to Greas - y Lake?   It's about a mile down on the dark side of

friend G - man, all dud -ed up for Sat - ur - day night.
Route Eighty - Eight, I got a bot -tle of rose, so let's try it.

Well,
We'll pick up Haz - y Da - vy and Kill - er Joe, and I'll

take you all out to where the gyp - sy an - gels go.   They're built like light,

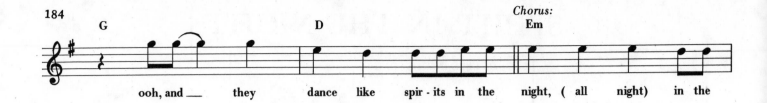

ooh, and __ they dance like spir-its in the night, (all night) in the

night." (all __ night) Oh ya don't know what they can do to ya, Spir-its in the

night, (all night) oh in the night, (all __ night) stand right up now and let her shoot

through ya. Well, now

Verse 2:
Wild Billy was a crazy cat,
And he shook some dust out of his coon skip cap,
He said "Trust some of this, it'll show you where you're at,
Or at least it'll help you really feel it."
By the time we made it up to Greasy Lake,
I had my head out the window, and Janey's fingers were in my cake.
I think I really dug her, well, I was to loose to fake.
I said, "I'm hurt." She said, "Honey, let me heal it."
And we danced all night to a soul fairy band,
And she kissed me just right like only a lonely angel can.
She felt so nice, just as soft as a spirit out of night,...

(To Chorus:)

Verse 3:
Now the night was bright and the stars threw lights
On Billy and Davy dancin' in the moonlight.
They were down near the water in a stone mud fight,
Killer Joe gone passed out on the lawn.
Well, now Hazy Davy got really hurt,
He ran into the lake in just his socks and a shirt.
Me and Crazy Janey was makin' love in the dirt,
Singin' our birthday songs.
Janey said it was time to go,
So we closed our eyes and said goodbye to gypsy angel row.
Felt so right, together we moved like spirits in the night...

(To Chorus:)

STAND ON IT

CHORDS USED IN THIS SONG:

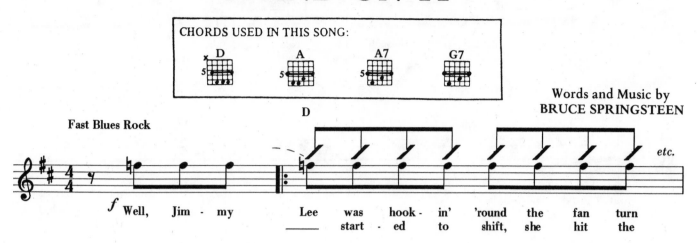

Words and Music by
BRUCE SPRINGSTEEN

Fast Blues Rock

Well, Jim - my Lee was hook - in' 'round the fan turn
_____ start - ed to shift, she hit the

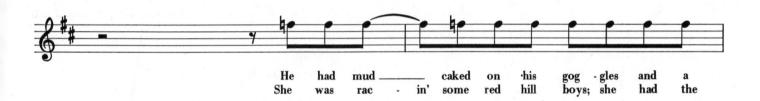

of a funk - y South - ern Flor - 'da dirt track.
shift, but she just could - n't get a hand on it.

He had mud _____ caked on his gog - gles and a
She was rac - in' some red hill boys; she had the

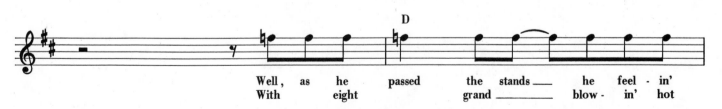

scream - in' three fif - ty stacked up on his back.
deed to the ranch, and a grand on it.

Well, as he passed the stands _____ he feel - in'
With eight grand _____ blow - in' hot

all   tuck - ered   out, ___   when through   the   roar   of   his   en - gine   he   heard
on   the   red   line, ___   she blew   past   a   hitch - hik - er   out   on

some - bod - y shout. ___   } "Stand ___   on ___ it.   Come on ___ boy,
route Thir-ty   nine, he hollered   (baby)

1.2.3.4.   **5.**

stand   on ___ it."   Mar - y   Beth ___

Repeat at lib and fade

Stand   on ___ it.   Come on _ boy,   stand   on _ it!   Come on _ man,

(Chorus:)
Well, now when it doubt and you can't figure it out,
Just stand on it.
Well, if your minds confused; you don't know what you're gonna do,
Well buddy, stand on it!
Well if you've lost control of the situation at hand,
Go grab a girl; go see a rock n' roll band,
And stand on it.
Come on man, stand on it!

Verse 3:
Well now, Columbus, he discovered America
Even though he hadn't planned on it.
He got lost, and woke up one morning
When he's about to land on it.
He wouldn't have got out of Italy man, that's for sure,
Without Queen Isabella standing on the shore shouting,
"Stand on it! Go ahead man, stand on it."

(Repeat Chorus:)

STATE TROOPER

CHORDS USED IN THIS SONG:

Words and Music by
BRUCE SPRINGSTEEN

188

Chorus:

- ter state troop - er, please____

don't stop me.   Please____ don't stop me.

D

Am

Please____ don't stop me.

1.2.   D.C.   3.

Verse 3:
Maybe you got a kid,
Maybe you got a pretty wife.
The only thing that I got's
Been bothering me my whole life.

(Chorus:)

Verse 4:
In the wee, wee hours,
Your mind gets hazy.
Radio relay towers
Lead me to my baby.

Verse 5:
The radio's jammed up
With talk show stations.
It's just talk, talk, talk
Till you lose your patience.

(Chorus:)

STOLEN CAR

Words and Music by
BRUCE SPRINGSTEEN

190

1. **2.3.**

I'm driv - ing a stol - en car___
ride by night___

down on El - dridge Av - e - nue.
and I trav - el in fear

Each night___ I
that in___ this

C(9)

wait to get caught,
dark - ness,

G

but I nev - er do.___
I will dis - ap - pear.___

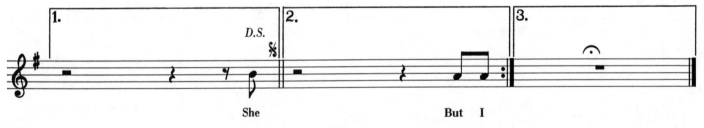

1. **2.** **3.**

D.S.

She But I

Verse 3:
She asked if I remembered the letters I wrote
When our love was young and bold.
She said last night she read those letters
And they made her feel one hundred years old.

(Chorus:)

STREETS OF FIRE

Words and Music by
BRUCE SPRINGSTEEN

Slow Rock

When the

night's quiet and you don't care an - y - more — and your
wan - der - ing a los - er down the track and I'm

eyes are tir - ed, and there's some - one at your door, — and you
dy - ing but babe I can't go back 'cause in the

re - al - ize you wan - na let go. —
dark - ness I heard some - bod - y call my name. —

And the weak lies — and the
And when you re - al - ize

cold walls you em - brace eat at your in - sides — and
how they tricked you this time, and it's all lies, — but I'm

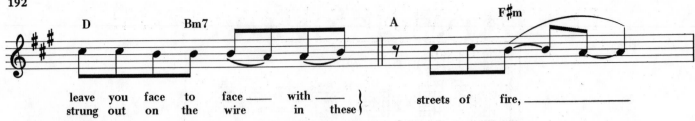

leave you face to face ____ with ____ streets of fire, ____
strung out on the wire in these } streets of fire, ____

streets of fire, ____ streets of fire, ____

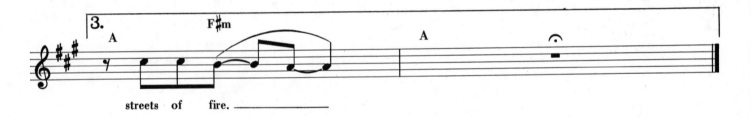

1. streets of fire. ____ Now I'm | **2.** *D.C.*

3. streets of fire. ____

Verse 3:
I live now only with strangers
I talk to only strangers,
I walk with angels that have no place.

TENTH AVENUE FREEZE-OUT

CHORDS USED IN THIS SONG:

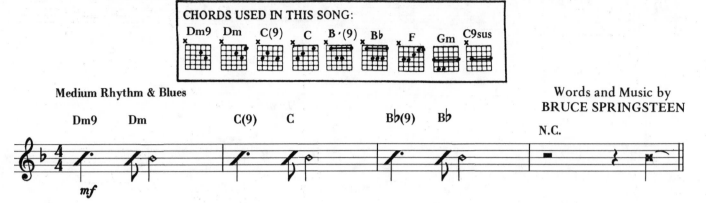

Dm9 Dm C(9) C B♭(9) B♭ F Gm C9sus

Medium Rhythm & Blues

Words and Music by
BRUCE SPRINGSTEEN

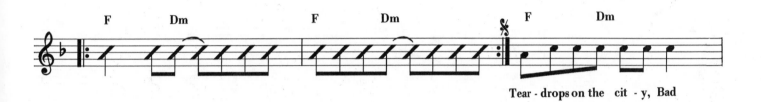

Dm9 Dm C(9) C B♭(9) B♭ N.C.

mf

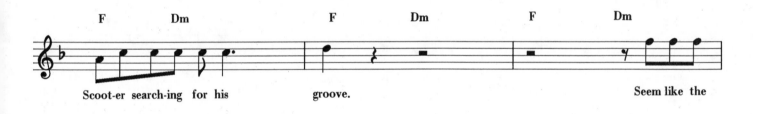

F Dm F Dm F Dm

Tear - drops on the cit - y, Bad

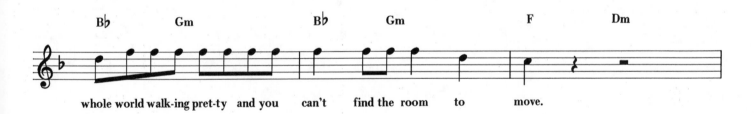

F Dm F Dm F Dm

Scoot-er search-ing for his groove. Seem like the

B♭ Gm B♭ Gm F Dm

whole world walk-ing pret-ty and you can't find the room to move.

F Dm C

Well, eve - ry - bod -y bet-ter move o - ver, that's all, _____ 'cause I'm

B♭

run -ning on the bad side and I got my back to the wall. _____

Tenth Av - e - nue   freeze   out! ____   Tenth Av - e - nue

1. F   Dm   *D.S.* **2.** F   Dm   *To next strain* **3.** F   Dm   *Repeat and fade*

freeze - out! ____   Well, I was   freeze - out! ____   And I'm freeze - out! ____

Dm9   Dm   C(9)   C   Bb(9)   Bb

all   a - lone, ____   I'm all a - lone. ____   And I'm

Dm9   Dm   C(9)   C   Bb(9)   Bb   C9sus

on   my   own, ____   I'm on my   own,   and I can't   go

D.S.

F   Dm   F   Dm   F   Dm   F   Dm

home. ____

Verse 2:
Well, I was stranded in the jungle trying to
Take in all the heat they was giving.
The night is dark, but the sidewalk's bright
And lined with the light of the living.
From a tenement window a transistor blasts.
Turn around the corner, things got real quiet real fast
I walked into a Tenth Avenue freeze-out!

Verse 3:
When the charge was made uptown,
And the Big Man joined the band,
From the coastline to the city all the
Little pretties raise their hands.
I'm gonna sit back right easy and laugh
When the Scooter and the Big Man
bust this city in half with the
Tenth Avenue freeze-out!

THE ANGEL

Words and Music by
BRUCE SPRINGSTEEN

The an - gel rides with hun - backed chil - dren; poi - son ooz - ing from his en - gine, wield - in' love as a le - thal wea - pon, on his way to hub - cap heav - en. Base - ball whore. bones. ——

Bridge:

Mad - i - son Av - e - nue's claim to fame

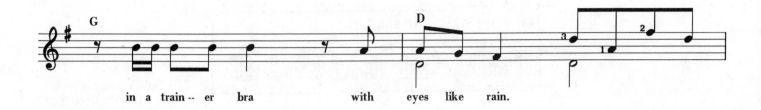

in a train -- er bra   with   eyes like rain.

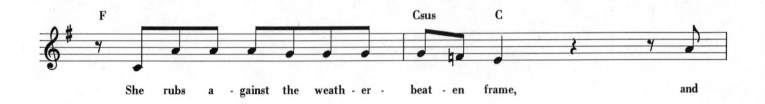

She rubs a - gainst the weath - er - beat - en frame,   and

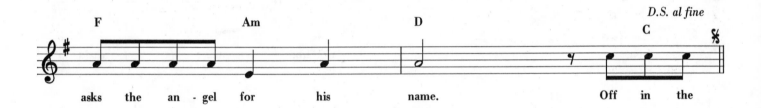

asks   the an - gel   for   his   name.   Off   in   the

Verse 2:
Baseball cards poked in his spokes,
His boots in oil, he's patiently soaked.
The roadside attendant nervously jokes
As the angel's tires stroke his precious pavement.

Verse 3:
The interstate's choked with nomadic hordes
In Volkswagen vans with full running boards
Dragging great anchors.
Followin' dead-end signs into the sores,
The angel rides by humpin' his hunk metal whore. *(To Bridge:)*

Verse 4:
Off in the distance the marble dome
Reflects across the faltlands
With a naked feel off into parts unknown.
The woman strokes his polished chrome
And lies beside the angel's bones.

THE E STREET SHUFFLE

CHORDS USED IN THIS SONG:

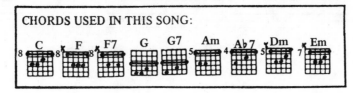

Words and Music by
BRUCE SPRINGSTEEN

Moderate R & B

mf (Rhthm Guitar)

(simile)

Sparks fly on "E"___ street when the boy - pro-phets walk it hand-some and hot.

All the lit - tle girls' souls ___ go weak when the man - child gives them a dou -

ble shot. The school - boy pops pull out all the stops ___

on a Fri - day night. _____ The teen -

C

___ age tramps in skin - tight pants do the "E" street dance and

G

ev - ery - thing's al - right. ___ Lit - tle kids ___ down there ei - ther danc-ing or

Am

hooked up in a scuf - fle dressed in snake - skin suits ___ packed with

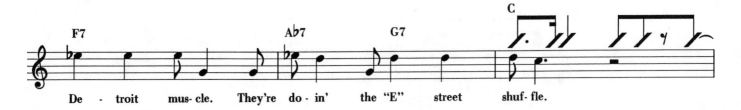

F7   Ab7   G7   C

De - troit mus- cle. They're do - in' the "E" street shuf- fle.

1.   2.3.

Fine

Am

Lit - tle An - gel says, "Oh, oh, ___

ev - ery - bod - y form a line. _____ Oh, _____

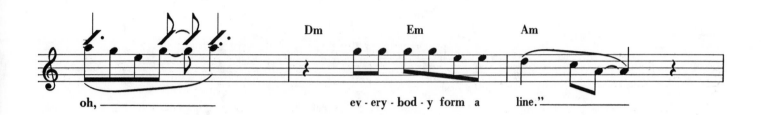

oh, _____ ev - ery - bod - y form a line." _____

Em   Dm   G7   D.S. al Fine

Verse 2:

Now those E Street brats in twilight duel flashlight phantoms
 in full star stream,
Down fire trails on silver nights with blonde girls pledged
 sweet sixteen.
The newsboys say the heat's been bad since Power Thirteen gave
 a trooper all he had in a summer scuffle,
And Power's girl, Little Angel, been on the corner keepin' those
 crazy boys out of trouble.
Little Angel steps the shuffle like she ain't got no brains,
She's deaf in combat down on Lover's Lane.
She drives all them local boys insane,

Verse 3:

Sparks fly on E Street when the boy-prophets walk it handsome
 and hot.
All them little girls' souls go weak when the manchild gives
 them a double shot.
Little Angel hangs out at Easy Joe's. It's a club where all the
 riot squad boys when they're cashin' in for a cheap hustle,
But them bous are still on the corner loose and doin' that lazy
 E Street Shuffle.
As them sweet summer nights turn into summer dreams Little Angel
 picks up Power and he slips on his jeans as they move on out
Down to the scene, all the kids are dancin'.

THE FEVER

THE PRICE YOU PAY

Words and Music by
BRUCE SPRINGSTEEN

Verse 3:
Now they'd come so far and they'd waited so long,
Just to end up caught in a dream where everything goes wrong,
Where the dark of night holds back the light of the day,
And you've gotta stand and fight for the price you pay.

(Chorus:)

Verse 4:
Little girl down on the strand, with that pretty little baby in your hands,
Do you remember the story of the promised land;
How he crossed the desert sands and he could not enter the chosen land?
On the banks of the river he stayed to face the price you pay.

Verse 5:
So let the game start. You better run, you little wild heart.
You can run through all the nights and all the days.
But just across the countyline, a stranger passin' through put up a sign.
That counts the men fallen away to the price you pay.
And girl, before the end of the day,
I'm gonna tear it down and throw it away.

THE PROMISED LAND

Pret-ty soon ___ lit-tle girl I'm gon - na take charge. The
find some-bod-y itch-ing for some - thing to start.

Chorus:

dogs on Main Street howl, 'cause they un-der-stand ___ if I could

take one mo-ment in - to my hands. ___ Mis-ter I ain't a boy, no

I'm ___ a man and I be - lieve in the Prom - ised Land.

Prom - ised Land. Prom - ised Land, and I be - lieve in the

Prom - ised Land, and I be - lieve in the Prom - ised Land.

Verse 3:
There's a dark cloud rising from the desert floor
I pack my bags and I'm heading straight into the storm.
Gonna be a twister that blows everything down
That ain't got the faith to stand its ground.
Blow away the dreams that tear you apart.
Blow away the dreams that break your heart.
Blow away the lies that leave you nothing
But lost and broken hearted.

(Chorus:)

THE RIVER

Words and Music by
BRUCE SPRINGSTEEN

come from down in the valley where, mis-ter, when you're
I got Mar-y preg-nant and, man,that was all she

young, they bring you up to do
wrote. And for my nine-teenth birthday I got a union

like your dad-dy done._____ Me and Mar-y, we met in high__
card and a wed-din' coat._____ We went down to the court-

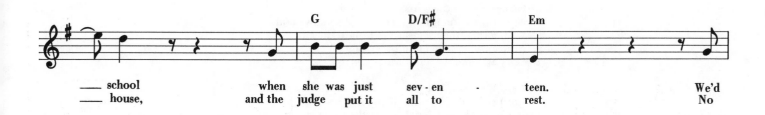

__ school when she was just sev-en-teen. We'd
__ house, and the judge put it all to rest. No

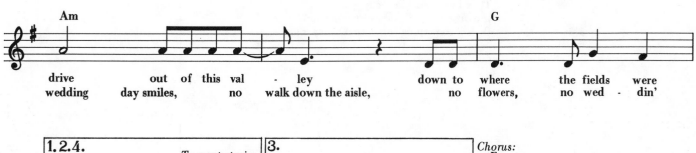

drive out of this val-ley down to where the fields were
wedding day smiles, no walk down the aisle, no flowers, no wed-din'

1.2.4. *To next strain* | 3. | *Chorus:* Em *etc.*

C | C

green. We'd go care but I re-down to the
dress. That night we went

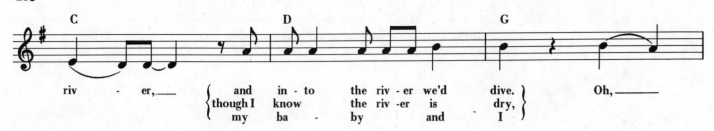

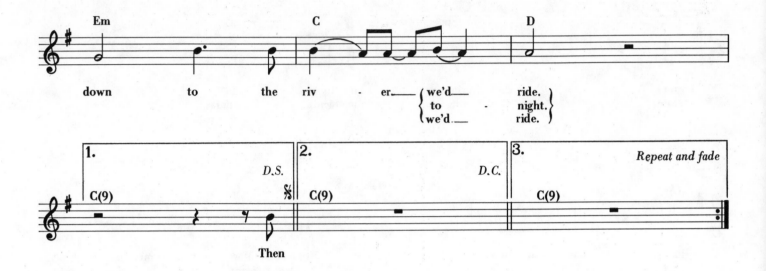

riv - er,____ {and in - to the riv-er we'd dive. / though I know the riv-er is dry, / my ba - by and I} Oh,____

down to the riv - er____ {we'd____ ride. / to - night. / we'd ____ ride.}

Then

Verse 3:
I got a job working construction
For the Johstown Company,
But lately there ain't been much work
On account of the economy.
Now all of them things that seemed so important
Well, mister, they vanished right into the air.
Now I just act like I don't remember.
Mary acts like she don't care.

Verse 4:
But I remember us ridin' in my brother's car,
Her body tan and wet down at the reservoir.
At night on them banks I'd lie awake and put her close
Just to feel each breath she'd take.
Now those mem'ries come back to haunt me.
They haunt me like a curse.
Is a dream a lie if it don't come true?
Or is it something worse that sends me...

(To Chorus:)

THE TIES THAT BIND

Words and Music by
BRUCE SPRINGSTEEN

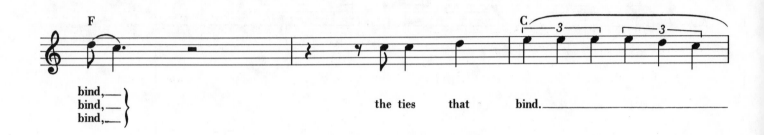

by, but you're walk - in' blind_____ to the ties____ that
dar -lin', can you walk____ the line_____ and face the ties____ that
dar-lin', we will stand____ in line_____ to face the ties____ that

bind,__ ⎫
bind,__ ⎬   the ties   that   bind._____
bind,__ ⎭

Now you   can't

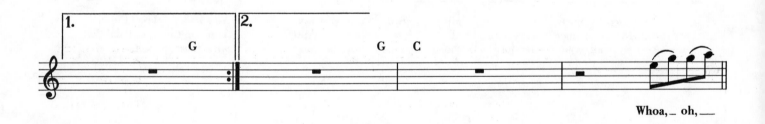

break_____   the ties   that   bind._____

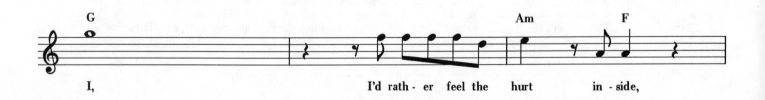

I,   I'd rath - er feel the hurt   in - side,

yes, I would, dar - lin', than know, _____

than know the emp- ti - ness your heart must hide. Yes, I would, dar - lin'.

Yes, I would, dar - lin'. Yes, I would, oh ba - by.

D.C. al Coda

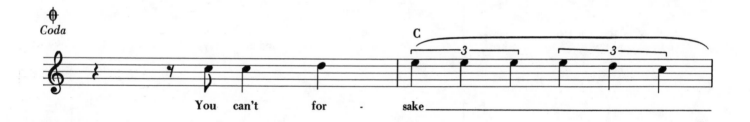

Coda

You can't for - sake _____

_____ the ties___ that bind._____ Whoa,_ whoa,_

oh. _____

THIS LITTLE GIRL

CHORDS USED IN THIS SONG:

Words and Music by
BRUCE SPRINGSTEEN

Chorus:

This lit-tle girl is mine,____ oh,____ this lit-tle girl is mine.__

____ Oh,____ this lit-tle girl, this____ lit-tle girl, this__

____ lit-tle girl____ is mine.____ Oh,____ ____ 2. Well, if the

____ 3.Hey, you bet-ter watch ____

Verse 3:
Hey, you better watch out!
I'm tellin' you the score.
Are you gonna be sweepin'
Your broken heart up off the floor?
Oh, and that ain't all,
I'm tellin' you, my friend.
I know what's on your mind,
Know what you wanna do.
But if you mess with her,
I'm gonna mess with you.
You like the way she moves,
You like to watch her walk.
You better listen up,
'Cause, man, this ain't just talk.
You better watch yourself,
You better stay in line.
Now, mister, I said,

(To Chorus:)

THUNDER ROAD

Words and Music by
BRUCE SPRINGSTEEN

215

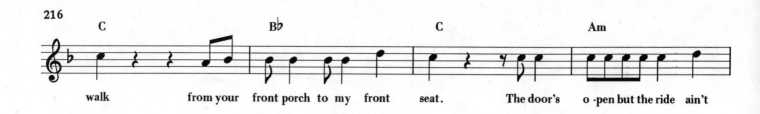

walk from your front porch to my front seat. The door's o -pen but the ride ain't

free; and I know you're lone-ly for words that I ain't spo - ken but to-

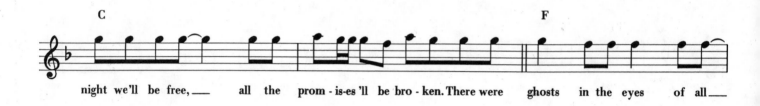

night we'll be free, ___ all the prom - is-es 'll be bro - ken. There were ghosts in the eyes of all ___

the boys ___ you sent a - way. They haunt this dust-y beach road _ in the

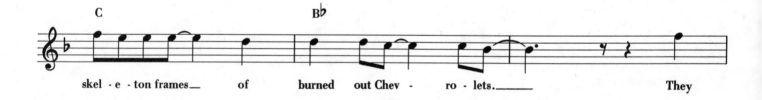

skel - e - ton frames ___ of burned out Chev - ro - lets. ___ They

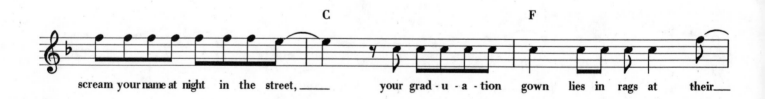

scream your name at night in the street, ___ your grad - u - a - tion gown lies in rags at their ___

___ feet. And in the lone - ly cool ___ be - fore dawn, ___ you hear their

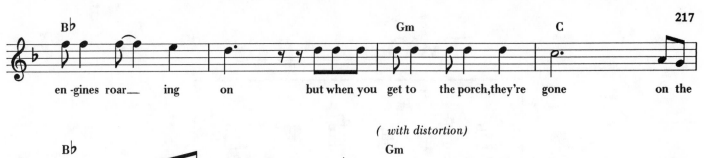

en-gines roar___ ing   on   but when you get to   the porch,they're gone   on the

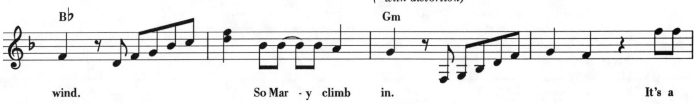

(with distortion)

wind.   So Mar - y climb   in.   It's a

town full of los-ers,___   I'm   pull-ing out of here to win._____

Repeat and fade

Instrumental Solo

Verse 2:
Don't run back inside darling, you know just what I'm here for.
So you're scared and your thinking that maybe we ain't that young anymore.
Show a little faith, there's magic in the night. You ain't a beauty but hey you're alright.
Oh, and that's alright with me.

Verse 3:
You can't hide 'neath your covers and study your pain,
Make crosses from your lovers, throw roses in the rain,
Waste your summer praying in vain
For a savior to rise from these streets.

Verse 4:
Well now, I'm no hero that's understood.
All redemption I can offer girl is beneath this dirty hood
With a chance to make it good somehow.
Hey, what else can we do now?

Verse 5:
Except roll down the window and let the wind blow back your hair.
Well, the night's busting open, these two lanes will take us anywhere.

Verse 6:
Oh, come take my hand, riding out tonight to case the promised land.
Oh, Thunder Road, oh, Thunder Road, oh Thunder Road.

Verse 7:
Lying out there like a killer in the sun,
Hey I know it's late, we can make it if we run.
Oh, Thunder Road, sit tight, take hold, Thunder Road.

Verse 8:
There were ghosts in the eyes of all the boys you sent away.
They haunt this dusty beach road in the skeleton frames
Of burned out Chevrolets
They scream your name at night in the street,
Your graduation gown lies in rags at their feet.

TWO HEARTS

Words and Music by
BRUCE SPRINGSTEEN

219

Some-day____ your cry - ing, girl,____ will end.____
to be - come a man____ and grow up to dream____ a - gain.____
That's why I'll ____ keep search - ing till ____ I find ____

Chorus:

And you'll find once a - gain____
I be - lieve in the end,____ } Two
my spe - cial one.____ }
lieve ____ }

hearts are bet - ter than one. Two hearts, girl, get the job

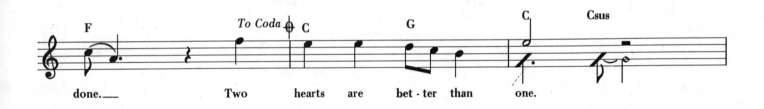

To Coda

done.____ Two hearts are bet - ter than one.

1.   2. *To next strain*   3.   *D.S.S.* al Coda

Some   I ____ be -

times it might____ seem like it was planned____ for you to roam____ emp - ty

heart - ed   through___ this   land._____ Though the world turns you

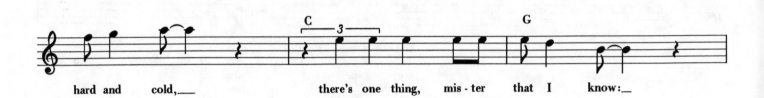

hard and   cold,___   there's one thing, mis - ter that I   know:__

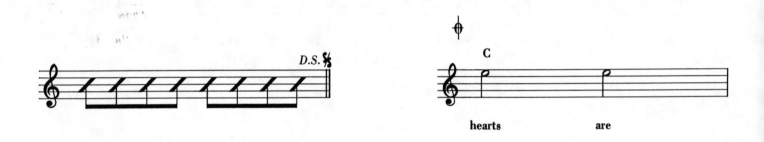

hearts   are

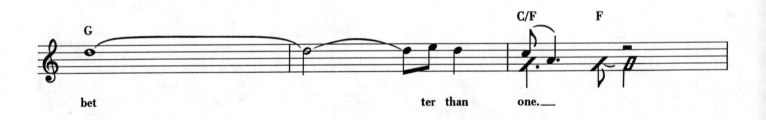

bet   ter than   one.__

USED CARS

CHORDS USED IN THIS SONG:

Moderate Folk Style

Words and Music by
BRUCE SPRINGSTEEN

mf

(fingerpicking)

My lit -tle

(simile)

sis - ter's   in the front seat   with an   ice   cream   cone;
ma she   fin - gers   her   wed - ding   band,

my ma's___ in the back___ seat sit - tin'   all   a -
and watch - es   the sales-man stare   at my   old   man's

lone   as my pa   steers her   slow___ out
hands.   He's tellin'   us all about the   break he'd   give___ us if he

of   the lot_____   for a   test drive_____ down Mich-i-gan
could but he just___ can't.

1.3.

2.4.

Av - e - nue.   Now, my   Well, if I could,___

I swear____ I know just what I'd do.____ Now

mis - ter, the day the lot - ter-y I____ win____ I ain't ev -

- er gon - na ride in no used car____ a - gain.

1.

D.S. 2.

Now, the

Verse 2:
Now the neighbors come from near and far
As we pull up in our brand new used car.
I wish he'd just hit the gas and let out a cry,
Tell 'em all they can kiss our asses good-bye.
My dad, he sweats the same job from mornin' to morn.
Me, I walk home on the same dirty streets where I was born.
Up the block I can hear my little sister in the front seat blowin' that horn,
The sound echoin' all down Michigan Avenue
Now, mister, the day my number comes in,
I ain't ever gonna ride in no used car again.

WILD BILLY'S CIRCUS SONG

Words and Music by
BRUCE SPRINGSTEEN

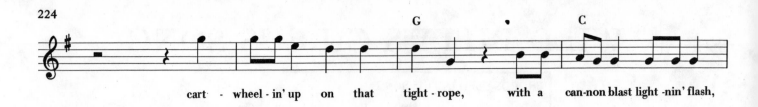

cart - wheel - in' up on that tight - rope, with a can-non blast light -nin' flash,

mov - in' fast through the tent, Mars bent, he's gon - na miss his fall,

oh God save the hu -man can - non ball. And the

fly - ing Zam - bi - nis watch Mar - guar - i - ta do her neck twist.

And the ring - mas - ter gets the crowd to count a - long, "Nine- ty -

five, nine -ty six, nine -ty se - ven." A rag - ged suit - case in his hand, he steals

si - lent - ly a - way from the cir - cus grounds. And the

kids, _past the sail - ors,_ to his dim - ly lit ____ trail -

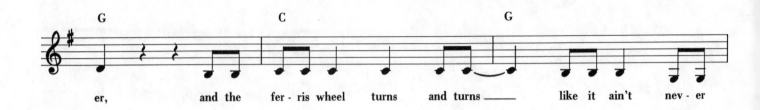

er, and the fer - ris wheel turns and turns ____ like it ain't nev - er

gon - na stop. And the cir - cus boss leans o - ver, whis- pers

in the lit - tle boy's ear, "Hey son, you want to try the big top?"

All a - board, Ne- bras - ka's our next stop.

Verse 2:
Well the runway lies ahead like a great false dawn,
Fat lady, big mama, Missy Bimbo sits in her chair and yawns,
And the man-beast lies in his cage sniffin' popcorn,
And the midget licks his fingers and suffers Missy Bimbo's scorn
Circus town's been born.

Verse 3:
And circus boy dances like a monkey on barbed wire,
And the barker romances with a junkie, she's got a flat tire,
And now the elephants dance real funky and the band plays like a
   jungle fire,
Circus town's on the live wire.
And the. . .

WORKING ON THE HIGHWAY

CHORDS USED IN THIS SONG:

Words and Music by
BRUCE SPRINGSTEEN

Bright Rock ♩ =176

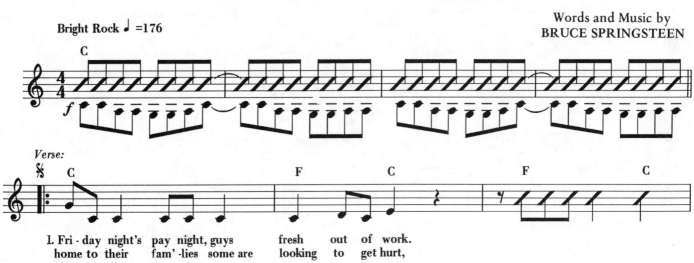

1. Fri - day night's pay night, guys fresh out of work.
home to their fam' -lies some are looking to get hurt,

Talk - ing 'bout the week - end, scrub -bing off the dirt.
some going _____ down to Stovell wearing trou - ble on their shirts.

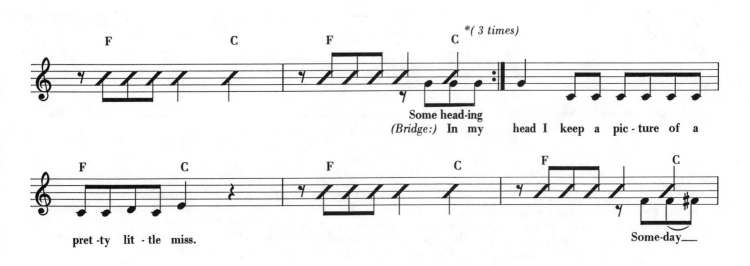

*(3 times)

Some head-ing
(Bridge:) In my head I keep a pic - ture of a

pret -ty lit - tle miss.
Some-day _____

(* - Repeat 3 times during lst verse only)

Mis - ter I'm gon - na lead a bet - ter life than this.

Work - ing on the high - way lay -
Work - ing on the high - way blast -

ing down the black - top. Work - ing on the high - way, all_____ day long I don't stop.
ing through the bed - rock. Work - ing on the high - way, work - ing on the high - way.

1st time D.S.
fine

3. (I)

Saved up my mon - ey and I put it all a - way; I went to see her dad - dy, but we

didn't have much to say. "Son, can't you see that she's just a lit - tle girl?

D.S. al fine

She don't know no-thin' 'bout this cruel, cruel world!"_____ 4. We lit

Verse 2:
I work for the county out on 95
All day I hold a red flag and watch the traffic pass me by.
In my head I keep a picture of a pretty little miss.
Someday, Mister, I'm gonna lead a better life than this.

Verse 3:
I met her at a dance down at the union hall.
She was standing with her brothers, back up against the wall.
Sometimes we'd go walking down the union tracks.
One day I looked straight at her and she looked straight back.

Verse 4:
We lit out down to Florida; we got along all right.
One day her brothers came and got her and they took me in a black and white.
The prosecutor kept the promise that he made on that day,
And the judge got mad and he put me straight away.
I wake up every morning to the work bell clang.
Me and the warden go swinging on the Charlotte County road gang.

WRECK ON THE HIGHWAY

CHORDS USED IN THIS SONG:
A   D   E   Esus   F#m

Moderately

Words and Music by
BRUCE SPRINGSTEEN

(fingerpicking)

Last

night   I was out driv - ing,
blood and glass all o - ver.

com - ing home at the end of a work - ing day.
And there was no - bod - y there but me.

I was rid - ing a - long through the
As the rain tum - bled down hard

driz - zling rain on a de - sert - ed stretch of a coun - ty two - lane when I
and cold, I seen a young man ly - ing by the side of the road. He cried

came up - on a wreck on the high - way.
"Mis - ter, won't you help me, please?"

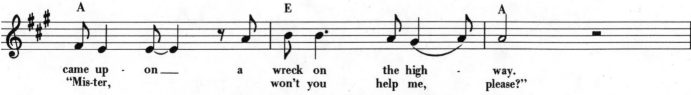

Now, there was

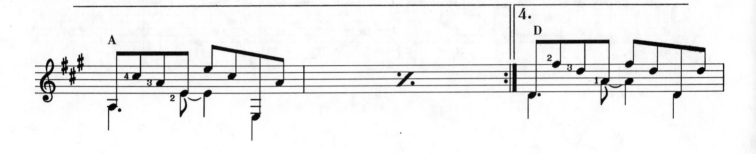

Verse 3:
An ambulance finally came and took him to Riverside.
I watched as they drove him away.
And I thought of a girlfriend or a young wife
And a State Trooper knocking in the middle of the night to say,
"Your baby died in a wreck on the highway."

Verse 4:
Sometimes I sit up in the darkness.
And I watch my baby as she sleeps.
Then I climb in bed and I hold her tight.
I just lay there awake in the middle of the night,
Thinking 'bout the wreck on the highway.

YOU CAN LOOK
(But You Better Not Touch)

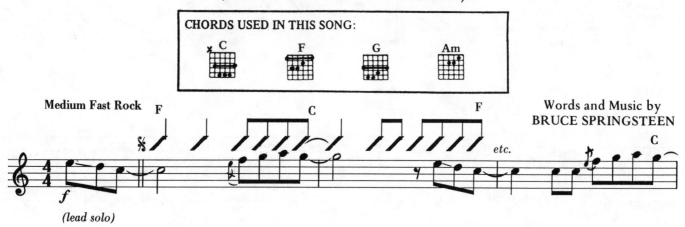

CHORDS USED IN THIS SONG:

Words and Music by
BRUCE SPRINGSTEEN

Medium Fast Rock

(lead solo)

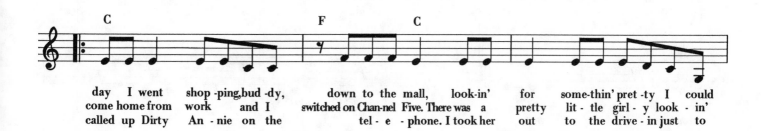

Well, yes -ter -
Well, I

day I went shop -ping, bud -dy, down to the mall, look -in' for some -thin' pret -ty I could
come home from work and I switched on Chan -nel Five. There was a pretty lit - tle girl - y look - in'
called up Dirty An - nie on the tel - e -phone. I took her out to the drive - in just to

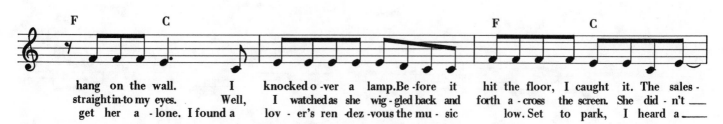

hang on the wall. I knocked o -ver a lamp. Be -fore it hit the floor, I caught it. The sales -
straight in-to my eyes. Well, I watched as she wig -gled back and forth a -cross the screen. She did - n't ___
get her a -lone. I found a lov - er's ren -dez -vous the mu - sic low. Set to park, I heard a ___

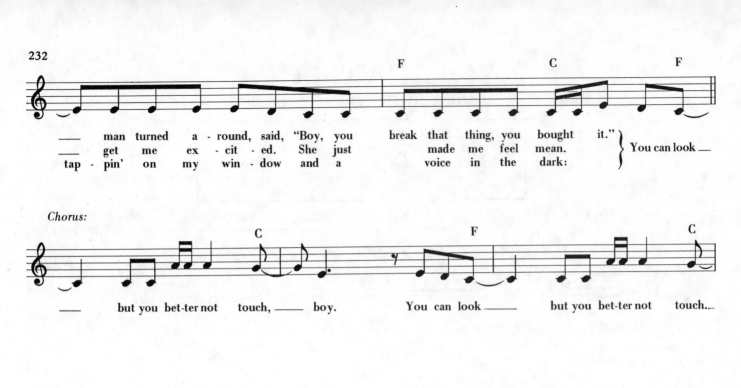

—— man turned a - round, said, "Boy, you break that thing, you bought it."
—— get me ex - cit - ed. She just made me feel mean.
tap - pin' on my win - dow and a voice in the dark:

You can look ——

Chorus:

—— but you bet-ter not touch, —— boy. You can look —— but you bet-ter not touch...

—— Mess a - round —— and you'll end up in dutch, —— boy. You can look —

—— but you bet - ter not, oh no, you bet - ter not, oh no, you bet - ter not

1. **2.** *D.S.* **3.**

(Lead solo)

touch. Well, I oh no, you bet - ter not

D.S. al Fine

oh no, you bet - ter not oh no, you bet - ter not...

(Lead solo)

INDEX OF FIRST LINES

INDEX OF FIRST LINES

INDEX OF FIRST LINES